Don't Downsize Your Dreams

Don't Downsize Your Dreams...

Leadership Inspiration for Women

Debbie Storey
Retired EVP, AT&T

Debbie Storey
Dallas, TX 75205
dstoreysg@aol.com
www.authordebbiestorey.com

Limits of Liability and Disclaimer of Warranty

The author and publisher shall not be liable for your misuse of this material. This book is strictly for informational and educational purposes.

Warning – Disclaimer

The purpose of this book is to educate and entertain. The author and/or publisher do not guarantee that anyone following these techniques, suggestions, tips, ideas, or strategies will become successful. The author and/or publisher shall have neither liability nor responsibility to anyone with respect to any loss or damage caused, or alleged to be caused, directly or indirectly by the information contained in this book.

ISBN-13: 978-1537772288
ISBN-10: 1537772287

About the Author

Debbie Storey has a passion for leading teams and making a difference for and through people.

Debbie is a retired executive from AT&T who spent most of her 34 years leading large organizations in various parts of BellSouth and AT&T operations. Her most recent role was EVP Mobility Customer Service, and prior to that, spent four years as Senior Vice President of Talent Development and Chief Diversity Officer at AT&T, responsible for identifying and developing leaders across 240,000 employees in 60 countries, aligning managers with the company's priorities, and driving employee engagement. She oversaw the award-winning AT&T University, as well as the company's efforts to leverage diversity and inclusion to drive innovation and growth.

She joined the company in 1982 as a clerk in a customer service department for a printing company that was later purchased by BellSouth. She held positions of increasing responsibility in customer service, sales, distribution, supply chain, operations, network, M&A, digital & social media, and HR, first at BellSouth and then AT&T.

Debbie has been a featured keynote speaker, moderator, and panelist at meetings and conferences throughout the country, where she has spoken on topics ranging from leadership and diversity to education and workforce transformation. She has been featured in print and digital media, including *Forefront Magazine*, *Business Digest* (France), *WE Magazine*, *Racing*

Toward Diversity, and *Profiles in Diversity*, as well as radio and TV interviews and numerous books on leadership, risk taking, and confidence.

A native of Boston, Debbie holds a Masters of Business Administration degree from UGA's Terry College of Business. Debbie serves on the Terry College Alumni Board and Dean's Advisory Council, the AT&T Performing Arts Center Board, and the Baylor Healthcare System Advisory Board.

Dedication

This book is dedicated to my son, Chad, who will always be the most important thing I ever did in my life, and to my husband, Jay, who changed my life with his unwavering love and support.

Acknowledgments

I wish to personally thank the following people for their contributions to my inspiration and knowledge and for the rich experiences throughout this career and life journey that taught me so much.

Buster Horne and Paul Hollinger, my earliest role models, mentors, and sponsors, who taught me the most important fundamental leadership lessons through their outstanding leadership.

Bill Snell, Richard Burns, Bob Daniel, and Mark Kieffer for being the most demanding and yet most inspiring bosses I had the good fortune to work for. They are outstanding leaders who don't just create followers, they create other leaders. They each saw things in me and gave me opportunities when I wasn't even sure I was ready. I am extremely indebted to them for the impact they had on my evolution as a leader and on my career.

There are so many colleagues that I have worked with and crossed paths with in the course of my career who helped me find and hone my passion for leading people. I started to list them all but there isn't enough time or space so I will simply say that I feel blessed to have known you. You know who you are—thank you for being my muses, mentees, mentors, sounding boards, partners, antagonists, role models, and inspiration.

I could never have written this book without the personal support and encouragement of three sisters and their beautiful, wonderful families. You never judge or question whether something is possible, you only give love and unwavering confidence that we can tackle anything as long as we stick together. I love you all.

I'd also like to thank the people without whose expertise, guidance, and insight I would not have even known how to get this book on paper. Donna Kozik, book coach extraordinaire. Jamie Gifford, so much more than just a proofreader. Deanna Newsome, production coordinator, and Susan Veach, cover design. This is the amazing team who enable words on pages to come alive as a published book.

Last here but first in my life, I'd like to give thanks to God who has shown me time and again that those who leave everything in God's hands will eventually see God's hands in everything.

Contents

Chapter 1:
Early Inspiration

Many years ago, early in my career, I was offered a ticket to the Possible Woman Conference in Atlanta. As a recent college graduate and new to the corporate world, it was a great opportunity and honor to meet other aspiring women and hear from successful leaders in Corporate America. I was ecstatic.

I was working for a telephone directory printing company on the south side of Atlanta at the time. It was basically a factory, a large manufacturing operation in a building pieced together to hold massive printing presses and more offices as the company grew.

Although I loved what I did and was excited to have my first job in Corporate America, it was far from glamorous. Much of my time was spent on the manufacturing floor walking among the noisy printing presses and delivering reports and schedules to press foremen, all in an environment in which everything was always covered in a fine layer of ink and paper dust.

At that point in my career I had no opportunity to interact with senior leaders of our business; it was actually intimidating to me to think I might run into one of them in the hall. That's how low I was on the totem pole. So the opportunity to dress up, drive downtown, and participate in a conference of "professional" women was beyond thrilling to me.

I felt like I had been given a ticket to step through the looking glass and see an entire new world. I couldn't wait to be sitting in that audience and just be *in close proximity* to women who had risen to the top against what were then, and continue to be now, pretty tough odds.

I had never heard an executive speak about their career journey before, and listening to these leaders opened up an entire new world of possibility to me. I sat in that big auditorium and listened in awe to the speakers on the stage—successful women who had "made it." I believe everyone has a spark inside them that, with the right inspiration, can become a burning flame. That first conference found the spark in me and turned it into an inferno.

I was so energized and motivated by the career stories and insights these successful women shared, their words of inspiration to all of us in that audience, and I wanted more.

After that, I took advantage of every opportunity I could to attend leadership conferences. Those that featured not just local business "stars," but nationally renowned leaders and speakers. Both men and women spoke, but it was always the women whose message resonated with me, motivated me, and kept the fire burning within me.

Those female leaders shared their journeys and their stories and talked about the obstacles they overcame along the way to executive and CEO positions. They shared great tips on having confidence, getting out of your comfort zone, building a network. As they talked, I hung on every word and soaked it all in.

You see, up to this point I had thought of women who had made it all the way to the top as being somehow superhuman, different from the rest of us. But listening to these stories I began to believe that maybe they were more like us than I had imagined, maybe they were just real people who worked hard to get where they were, to the top of Corporate America.

Hearing about their climb to the C-suite, their struggles along the way, and their ultimate success, gave me something to aim for, and my dream of making it to the top was born. Their stories gave me hope, and I envisioned myself following in their footsteps. I thought, if they can do it, maybe I can too! They convinced me to dream big, and to hold on to that dream.

Those women were my role models, they were what I wanted to be, and listening to them made me believe that it was possible. Not only for me, but for other women, too. I thought of them as stars who were lighting the way, showing us the path so that all of us could follow.

Each time I heard one on stage, they inspired me to set goals, to keep pressing forward, to keep pursuing my passion. After every one of those conferences ended, I left with my batteries recharged. I would drive home and replay their stories over and over in my head. I would think about how I could use their insights and experiences to help me advance in my own career.

Sitting in the audience at that first conference, the Possible Woman Conference, I never imagined that one day I would be standing on a stage talking about my own career journey. But 28 years later, I found myself the keynote speaker for that exact same conference in Atlanta. I looked out at the audience where I had sat all those years ago and I told my story—how I started as a clerk in a customer service department of a printing company and survived two acquisitions, many business obstacles, and tremendous personal adversity to eventually rise to the position of Executive Vice President in a Fortune 10 company.

I had realized a dream that started long ago, a dream that was inspired by women who had shared their career stories and insights with aspiring women in the audience. So it is both an honor and a humbling experience to be able to tell my story here in these pages.

What I've learned through my own leadership journey is that those women who inspired me very early on from the stage weren't born smarter than anyone else, they weren't "different" or special, or even lucky. They were just the ones who had enough passion and courage to pursue their goals and persevere through adversity and obstacles. They were the ones who dared to imagine the possibilities, and then were never deterred in their journey to achieve their vision of success.

They dreamed big, and they never let anyone downsize their dreams.

My goal in the pages and stories that follow is to inspire you, challenge you, and motivate you. I want you to believe that it is absolutely possible to achieve success, no matter what your version looks like.

I dare you to imagine what is possible for YOU, and then never let anything cause you to downsize your dreams.

No matter what you've been through, no matter where you are going, no matter what your vision of success is, I dare you to keep that dream in front of you and to imagine all of the things life has to offer you.

Because, trust me when I tell you, my journey to this place and moment in life has not been without challenges and obstacles. My journey has taken lots of turns.

The one constant, the North Star that's guided me along the way and that I hope will guide you, has been that I never let obstacles downsize my dreams. I dared to imagine the possibilities, and I had role models who illuminated the path and inspired me to believe in the possibilities.

I have often said that the definition of "mentor" is someone whose hindsight can become your foresight.

I will share with you some of the lessons I've learned in hindsight that might become your foresight.

Because when I look back at my career, I can see with great clarity the things that worked. I wasn't knowledgeable enough to know the right things to do at the time—when I was early in my career no one talked about sponsorship or personal brands or networks—but in hindsight I can see clearly the key factors that led to my success. And I'm passionate about sharing that clarity and hindsight with you, illuminating the path for you to follow.

I can also see many of the things I did wrong, and I will share some of those as well so that you might avoid the landmines I stepped on at various stages of my career journey.

I want to begin by sharing with you what I believe were the four keys to my early success:

1. Made great coffee
2. Got in way over my head
3. Took big risks and failed in a very public way
4. Took a stand and put my family first

I'm guessing these don't sound like the conventional leadership tips you've heard before...but let me tell you how these things got me where I am today.

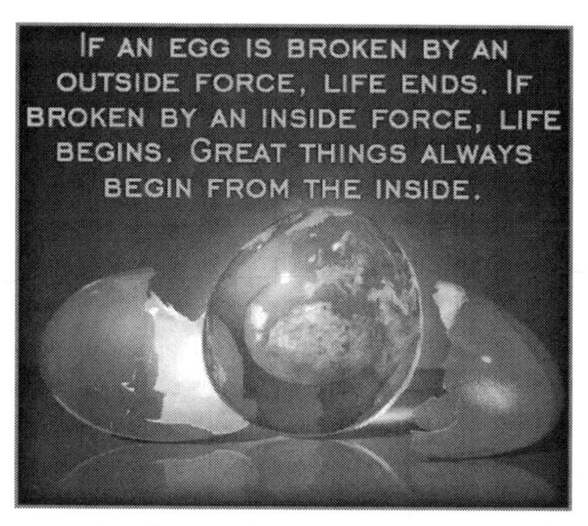

Great things are inside you...have the courage to unleash them.

Chapter 2: Made Great Coffee

I grew up in Atlanta in a fairly average, working class family with my parents and three younger sisters. My father had been in sales for one of the big oil companies and after having to uproot and relocate his young family every three or so years he was relocated to Atlanta. Three years went by and he was told his next move would be to Ohio, and he decided it was time to make a career change that would allow his family to stay settled in Atlanta. He became an entrepreneur and bought, ran, and sold businesses for the rest of his life.

The life and finances of an entrepreneur aren't always predictable, and during those years there were times when things were very good, and there were also some very lean times. During one of those lean years we were struggling to pay the bills, and my mom decided that she and I would go to work at McDonalds. I was in high school at the time, and the thought of working at McDonalds was appalling to me. But I didn't have a choice, and there we were, my mom and I, working side-by-side serving burgers and fries.

I was mortified to have any of my friends know that I was working at McDonalds, so every time someone I knew came into the restaurant I would immediately run and hide in the back by the fry machine. I would only come out after I was sure they had left the parking lot. After watching me do this over and over again, my mom finally caught me as I slunk back out to the front counter and she said, "What are you doing? Why do you care what other people think? Get over yourself. Just do what you need to do and let's have fun doing it!"

I learned a valuable lesson from my wonderful, smart, spirited mom that I would carry with me throughout my life—do whatever you're asked to do and find a way to have fun doing it.

After high school I attended the University of Georgia. I had to pay for many of my own expenses, so I worked in my dad's restaurant business all the way through college. I waitressed, washed dishes, and eventually managed my own restaurant.

After I graduated from college I continued to work for the restaurant corporation, helping with the oversight and management of six restaurants. The money was great, but the hours were grueling and the work wasn't glamorous. I got to travel around to all six restaurants every day to oversee operations and collect the money, but if a dishwasher didn't show up I also got to wash the dishes. I realized it wasn't where I wanted to build a career.

So I dreamed of the possibilities of a career in Corporate America.

I had graduated from the University of Georgia with a degree in Psychology and a minor in Criminal Justice, intending to go to law school until an internship in the court system changed my mind, so I still didn't know exactly what I wanted to be when I grew up. I didn't have a burning interest in a particular industry or company, so I decided to interview with a variety of companies in different industries, with the ultimate goal of shopping for a boss.

My experience in the restaurant business had taught me the importance of leadership and the distinct difference a boss can make on the culture, environment, and the success of a business. Each of the six restaurants I oversaw had a manager who was fully responsible for all operations within their restaurant—hiring, firing, processes, food preparation, special offers to get customers in the door. Their leadership and management style drove the culture and environment, and the profitability, in their restaurant.

The manager of one particular restaurant ruled with an autocratic style—he barked orders and dictated every aspect of the restaurant operations and the servers' interactions with customers. He yelled and ranted when something didn't go right. He docked workers' pay if they were more than a minute late to their shift. He micro-managed what every employee did, every minute of their shift. And I observed that people didn't like working there, the turnover was higher than in other restaurants and it was tougher to hire new employees. People only cared about not getting fired, they didn't love what they did and they weren't willing to go the extra mile because they knew they would receive no recognition for it. This manager drove his people hard and ruled with an iron fist, but sales and margins were lower in this restaurant than in any other restaurant.

The manager of another store led with a very different style. He treated every employee as if they were a critical partner in the business by engaging them in the success of the restaurant. He sought their input, he taught them everything he knew about running restaurants, he let them try new things, he praised them when things went well, and he treated honest mistakes as learning experiences. He shared information about sales numbers and food costs so they understood the impact they could make on the success of the business. He provided opportunities to learn and grow—people who started as dishwashers could work hard, learn, and be promoted to servers, and then to cooks, and then to assistant managers. He made it fun, engaging, and rewarding to work there. His sales and margins were higher than in any of the other six restaurants.

I wanted to work for a boss like that. I thought finding the right kind of leader was more important than just finding a job.

So I made up my mind that as I went through the interview process, I would focus more on finding the right boss than just jumping on any job offer I received.

I wanted to find the right fit in a company that shared my values and valued my work ethic. I wanted to find a boss who would mentor me, who would give me a chance to learn the business and develop my skills, and move up if I could prove myself.

I knew I had a lot to offer a company if I could find the right fit. Based on my experience and success in the restaurant business, I believed I had three qualities that would help me succeed in any environment. I've since come to think of these as the three "In" traits that as a leader I have always looked for in others:

1. Intelligence – a voracious appetite for learning with the capacity to get up to speed quickly, assimilate information, and see the big picture. The ability to deal with ambiguity and adapt to changing circumstances.
2. Intensity – the ability and willingness to dig in, do the hard work, do what is required to get the job done. The belief that there is always a way to achieve results and when one path is blocked there are multiple other paths that are still possible.
3. Integrity – the conviction to always do the right thing, set the right example, and deliver results in the right way. The belief that there is never, ever a right time do to the wrong thing.

It takes twenty years to build a reputation and five minutes to ruin it. If you think about that, you'll do things differently.

Warren Buffett, CEO of Berkshire Hathaway

Although I had a college degree and had been a VP/GM in the restaurant business, I decided to interview for entry level positions rather than try to bluff my way into a managerial position in a business or industry I didn't know. I really wanted to learn from the ground up and then advance into management positions with a strong foundation of knowledge.

In interview after interview I was told by the hiring manager that I was overqualified for the job. When I explained that I wanted to start at the bottom, learn a business from the ground up and then advance into leadership, some of the interviewers looked at me like I had two heads. In those interviews I could sense that not many employees at that company started at the bottom and were able to advance to management positions. I knew those leaders were not the boss I was looking for.

In one interview, I asked the manager to tell me about the opportunities employees in his organization had to pursue training and development and to move laterally into other opportunities in the company. He said, "Oh, we don't hire people who are interested in starting here, letting us train them, and then move on to other positions." I looked at *him* like he had two heads, and I wanted to end the interview there and run from his office. He called me a week after the interview to offer me the job. I considered it, I was getting worried at this point about finding a job, but when I thought about being trapped in one position, in one department, for many years I politely turned it down and continued my search.

I interviewed for months before I found the boss I wanted to work for. Paul Hollinger was the customer service manager of a telephone directory printing company whose biggest client was BellSouth.

Paul was looking for a clerk to support his customer service department. In the interview he didn't tell me I was overqualified for a job as a clerk. He actually asked me what my career aspirations were, where I hoped to be in five years, ten years. He was intrigued (rather than baffled) by the fact that I wanted to learn a business from the ground up. He offered insights on his leadership style and his experience and passion for developing people, without my even asking. Two minutes in, I knew this was the boss I had been looking for.

I didn't have any background or experience in the printing business, but at the end of our interview he offered me the job and committed to me that if I could work hard, learn fast, and demonstrate potential, he would help me advance in the company.

I accepted the job, and I eagerly anticipated the first day of my career in Corporate America and the opportunity to roll up my sleeves and begin learning and making a difference.

I remember vividly my first day on the job.

I showed up that first Monday looking forward to becoming a vital part of the customer service organization and providing what I envisioned as critical support activities like typing, filing, and maintaining records. But I was the first clerk they had ever had in the department, so when I asked my boss what I should get busy working on, I'll never forget his response. He said, "I'm not sure, we've never had a clerk before…

"…But why don't you start by making coffee."

I blinked once and wondered for a moment if he was joking. There was an awkward silence as he looked at me and wondered if he had made a mistake.

I looked back at him, and I had one of those moments when I said to myself, "What have I gotten myself into? Did he seriously just say my job is making coffee?"

I was a college graduate, I had been the VP/GM of a restaurant corporation, I didn't drink coffee, and I didn't even know the apparatus required to make it! Remember this was long before being a barista was cool. I had flashbacks to working at McDonald's with my mom.

But I took a breath and then smiled. In that moment, I decided if they asked me to make coffee, then I would make the best coffee ever, and I would have fun doing it (thanks Mom). I went to JC Penny and I asked a sales associate to help me purchase everything required to make coffee. I went back to the office and set up a little coffee station. And I made coffee. Great coffee.

But I didn't stop there.

I thought about it, and decided that rather than just make coffee and wait for more meaningful work to emerge, I'd take this opportunity to get to know people and learn about the business. I determined that a great way to do that would be to deliver a cup of coffee to my colleagues as they were getting settled in their offices in the morning. I was anxious to learn, and who could refuse to spend a few minutes with me if I went out of my way to deliver their coffee. So every morning I chose a different person to deliver coffee to, and I took that opportunity to engage, listen, and absorb all I could.

I have such vivid memories of those days as I delivered Styrofoam cups of coffee to cramped offices with creaky old desks littered with stacks of paper and glass ashtrays, a lit cigarette smoldering in most of them. Remember this was a telephone directory printing plant, 1982, and it was a facility that had been pieced together by buying adjacent buildings as the company grew. There were odd back staircases that led to some of the offices, little doors that looked like they should lead to hidden passages, and a fine layer of ink and paper dust covering every visible surface. I would carry a cup of coffee through those passages and staircases, dust off a chair in the office, and sit down to get to know people.

As I sat with a different person each morning, I would ask questions like "Tell me about your role here." "Who else do you interact with?" "How did you get where you are today?" "Where did you begin your career?" "If you could do it all over again, what would you do differently?" "If you were President for a day, what one thing would you change here?"

I listened, I learned, I made connections, and I soaked up every bit of knowledge I could.

As I learned more about the business, I began to ask people how I could help, and I began to make suggestions.

I dared to dream I could find a way to make myself invaluable, to demonstrate I was capable of a whole lot more than making great coffee.

For example, one morning I delivered coffee to John, and as I sat down to spend a few minutes with him I said, "I was talking with Ed last week and I noticed that he produces a report every day that has some of the same data on it that you go out and gather on your own every day. Maybe you could use Ed's report and save yourself some time."

John was thrilled that I had just made his job a little easier. And I was hooked. It felt great to be making a contribution, and I began looking for more ways that I could add value and make a difference.

And it worked.

Before long, I wasn't just making coffee, I was making copies! Then I was delivering daily instructions to the foreman on the manufacturing floor, then I was asked to deliver key daily production reports to senior managers, and then I actually started creating some of those key reports every day.

My to-do list grew, I was given new opportunities and challenges, and I was continuing to get to know people and to expand my network.

I was developing a reputation as someone who could be counted on to jump in, learn fast, do whatever was needed, and deliver above expectations.

In my six-month review, Paul Hollinger gave me feedback I remember to this day. He said, "You have taken the initiative to learn, you have done everything that was asked of you and done it skillfully and graciously, and you have exceeded everyone's expectations. You have made yourself an invaluable resource to this department and this company, and none of us can imagine what we would do without you."

He wasn't referring to my coffee-making skills. I was on my way to doing what I had set out to do—learn about a company and become an integral part of it from the ground up. I was ecstatic about the feedback and the recognition that I was making a difference.

And you know what, I kept *making great coffee.* Because that was part of my job. And that was part of my work ethic, to never say "not my job."

And six months after I joined the company as a clerk, I was promoted to a customer service representative.

Paul Hollinger had kept his word, and I had learned my first critical leadership lesson—

No matter what you are asked to do, do it better than anyone else.

If I had grumbled or shirked the responsibility of making coffee, I wouldn't have earned the opportunity to do more. If I hadn't found ways to make myself invaluable as a clerk, if I had spent all my time simply brown-nosing and trying to get promoted, I would not have cemented my reputation early on as a "go-to" person who could *always* be counted on to deliver.

No one "owes" you anything. Success, and reputations, have to be earned—by nailing your job, every single day. That is what earns you the right to do more, and the opportunity to advance.

Always Make Great Coffee

Chapter 3: Got In Over My Head

I worked hard, I did whatever was asked of me, and I built great relationships all across the company. I constantly took it upon myself to proactively learn all I could about the business, and I delivered results in every job and on every task I was given. I proved that I was capable of taking on increasingly bigger challenges.

I was fairly quickly promoted from customer service rep to supervisor to a manager, each role filled with broader responsibilities. I was so excited about the opportunities I had been given and gratified at how my career was progressing. I felt confident about the contributions I was making.

Paul Hollinger had eventually moved to another role and I had the opportunity and honor of stepping into his shoes as the customer service manager for the company. Having started as a clerk and learned the customer service work from the ground up, I had a great perspective on the opportunities that existed to streamline the work and shore up processes, making the work more efficient for our reps and the manufacturing operations. We implemented many improvements in customer service that increased productivity and accuracy and decreased the workload for the reps.

With our streamlined customer service processes in place, I realized that our team had the capacity to take on some of the extensive paperwork the sales team had to do to get our contracts with customers completed and work orders executed. Because our customer service reps had such a deep technical knowledge of the manufacturing operations, we were able to improve the accuracy and thoroughness of the contracts and work orders, which improved the accuracy of both our contractual commitments to customers and the final product.

It was a win/win for all of us—fewer errors for customer service to catch and fix in the manufacturing process, lower cost for the business, and higher customer satisfaction. The sales team loved the partnership and the elimination of some of the more manual work they used to have to do, and it freed them up to focus their energy on new sales development and forming tighter relationships with existing customers.

The partnership between customer service and sales was so effective that the sales team began asking us to go on customer visits with them, helping to further strengthen customer relationships and instill confidence in our ability to understand and meet their needs.

I loved the customer service work, loved my role, and felt we were making an increasingly significant contribution to the business. Everything was on track.

Until I got the call that challenged my confidence and made me weak in the knees. It turned out to be the first of many calls in my career where I was offered a job that I didn't feel I was qualified for, I didn't feel I had the experience or credentials to do.

I was a young woman, still in my twenties, in a completely male-dominated business.

The President called me in to his office for a meeting—I didn't have an opportunity to meet with the President very often so that alone was intimidating. He told me he was proud of my work, that I had done a fantastic job leading the customer service department, improving efficiency and reducing cost while improving accuracy. He told me he thought I was capable of making the same kinds of improvements in other areas of the business, and he asked me to take over sales for the company in addition to my current responsibilities. In other words, he wanted me to lead the sales team I had been working so closely with as a peer.

I wasn't sure I had heard him correctly. I'm sure I had a frozen smile on my face as my stomach dropped and I tried not to let him see my hands shaking. My mind was working fast but no words were coming out of my mouth.

I had been comfortable rising through the ranks of customer service and becoming the leader over an organization that I had worked my way up through. But he was asking me to do something I had never done before, to take over a department I had never even worked in. To step up and lead a team of my peers, to become a *boss* over this group of very seasoned men, each of whom had been selling printing contracts for close to three decades.

How could I possibly step into the role as their leader with any credibility at all?

I managed to keep my composure long enough to get out of his office and give myself time to process this curveball. I believe I said something about needing to give it some thought and discuss it with my family, and I walked out on shaky legs.

I left his office and immediately called one of my mentors, Frank, who was a senior leader in the company. I said, "I have a big problem. The President has asked me to take over the sales team and I need your help in figuring out the right way to say no. I don't have the background or experience to do this, I've never been in sales, I'm not qualified to step in and lead this team."

I will never forget his advice.

He said, "Do you think the President is offering you this role because you are an expert in sales?"

I said "No, he knows I don't have sales experience."

And he said, "You are being offered this job because you have established yourself as a great leader with a terrific reputation for delivering results. You've earned the respect of people all across this organization, and you have established relationships that enable you to get things done. I have confidence that you can do this, and there are so many people who will support you in this new role.

"You have earned this promotion. I know you're comfortable where you are, but *you need to get out of your comfort zone and have the confidence to say yes*."

He saw something in me that I didn't see, and he gave me the courage I needed to move away from what was comfortable and accept this new challenge. He gave me the confidence to get in way over my head.

He also gave me some critical advice as I became the new leader of this team of seasoned professionals who had previously been my peers.

He said, "Put yourself in their shoes. They know and respect you, but they know you're a strong leader who drives change. They might be skeptical about you coming in and trying to 'take over'—a young woman and a new sales leader trying to prove herself. You need to step into this role with humility—learn from them, show respect for what they know and do, and show that you're there to support them. There are changes that need to be made, but earn their trust before you begin to change the course of the work they have been doing for so many years."

So I prepared to step into my new role and take over the sales organization. I knew Frank was right, I had to earn their trust. I could envision them trying to help me fail if I just swooped into this seasoned group of professionals and acted like I knew their business and had all the answers.

So rather than come in with the list of things I thought we needed to address or change, right out of the gate I asked for their help and support.

On the day the announcement was made, I called them all together into a conference room—a large room that had one big wall of glass that overlooked the manufacturing floor. Imagine me, standing at the front of the room and looking around at these men, smoking cigarettes, gazing back at me through the rising smoke with skeptical looks on their faces.

I resisted the urge to run out the door and tell the President I changed my mind, that I was content where I was and just wanted to keep leading the customer service department. I took a big, deep breath and jumped in.

I told them how much I admired and respected the critical role they played in the corporation, that we wouldn't be where we were without the work they had done. I told them how much I had enjoyed working with them in my previous role, and I told them how excited I was about the opportunity to now be a part of this great team. And I told them I needed their help.

I told them I knew I had a lot to learn, and that I was counting on them to teach me.

I learned that a funny thing happens when you show humility and ask people for help. Their guard comes down, they don't think of you as something to be feared, and they get in the boat with you and are willing to help. And that's exactly what they did.

I spent time with each one of them over the next few weeks, letting them get to know my leadership style and at the same time learning the skills and motivations of each of them. They each shared with pride the work they were doing and the customers that were a part of their portfolio. They offered to let me shadow them as they met with customers. I asked a lot of questions so that I could quickly learn the mechanics and the nuances of their work.

I did my homework as well. I studied the sales and compensation processes. I poured over contracts and reviewed and analyzed the profitability of the work we were bringing in. I studied our historical sales trends and our forecasted sales. I looked at all the information I could find about what our competitors were doing. I talked with customers about what we did well and what we could do better.

I let the team know I was there to remove obstacles and support their success. I created some early wins—I asked them to tell me some of the things that were getting in the way of them doing their jobs and I fixed them. Low hanging fruit that earned the trust of the team and convinced them that I would make their work lives better and more productive.

Not all of them got on board immediately. There was one particular sales rep, I'll call him Al, who was the top selling rep, the Alpha Male and unofficial "leader of the pack." Al clearly didn't want me to interfere with what he did and stonewalled me at every turn. In my role as customer service manager, he had been the most challenging sales rep to deal with and we had butted heads over process issues more than once, so he was less than thrilled that I was now in the position of being his boss. He was never outright insubordinate, but made it clear that he didn't need or want my help or input.

The turning point with Al came when he was working to close a new, very large contract. I had to work hard to draw out any of the details of the negotiation with him, but Al had a big ego and I realized that if I asked him in our staff meeting to talk about his "big deal," he was willing to share *all* of the detail to impress the big team. In one of those sessions I gained some insight into the pricing obstacle that was keeping the deal from getting done, and I had an idea about a value-added service we might add, at almost no cost, to give ourselves an advantage over our competitor. I got approval from our CFO to include the service in the contract, and in our next staff meeting I put it on the table as the team discussed Al's big deal. The rest of the team loved it, they took the idea and expanded it, and Al realized it could be just the key to his closing the deal. Within a month, Al had a signed contract and a big bonus.

Al never thanked me for the idea or the help, I never tried to take the credit, but he knew that I had been instrumental in his ability to close that contract. His attitude toward me shifted, and over time we developed a terrific and very rewarding working partnership.

It wasn't easy, but I had earned the trust of the toughest member of the team and the rest of the team followed quickly. Earning their trust allowed me to manage them through the changes that were necessary in a way that engaged and energized them. We made significant improvements in the way we managed relationships with customers, the way we structured contracts, and the processes we followed to deliver work orders to the manufacturing plant. And we made changes in the way we collaborated together to help each other be successful.

We spent time together as a team, jointly creating a vision of where we wanted to drive sales over the next five to ten years. I asked them to get out of their comfort zones and think differently, creatively, about the business. I got them excited about the possibilities ahead of us, the opportunity to not just maintain the status quo, but to take some risks and expand our role in the business.

The most exciting change we made during that time, and one of the early highlights of my career, was working together to launch a new line of business for the company.

The company had idle capacity on our printing presses because there were natural peaks and valleys in the annual directory publishing cycle. The valleys left us with fixed costs to cover but no telephone directory work to fill it. The salesmen and I believed we had an opportunity to improve the overall profitability of the business if we could find work to consume that idle capacity.

The team came together to work on the challenge, a cohesive group of determined individuals all focused on the same mission. We would huddle together in the same conference room where I met with them all that first day, overlooking the manufacturing floor, working long into the night as we talked through ideas. And after a few weeks the plan came together—to go after a segment of independent telephone company printing, at lower pricing than our core telephone directory work, to fill our idle capacity.

Leadership now had to be convinced that it was the right direction for the business. Our team created business plans and white papers, ran pro-forma invoices and financials. We had to show that although this work would be priced at narrower margins than our core work, it would make a significant cash flow contribution to the business. Internal stakeholders had to be brought along as well to ensure that we could support this business that was different in some fundamental ways from our core business.

But our team was successful, we did it—ultimately launching a new line of business together that was a huge success and grew to almost 15% of the company's total revenue. That might not sound like a lot, but it was millions of dollars in revenue and made a big difference in the company's profitability.

So in spite of my initial fears about taking on a big role that I had no experience in, I grew and developed a new set of skills and credentials and led the team in a way that made a substantial contribution to the business.

Was it comfortable? No! There were many, many nights that I went home and thought to myself—I'm not sure I can pull this off, I have so much to learn, I'm in way over my head.

But I did pull it off. It took a lot of work, a lot of sweat, and a lot of humility. But I had learned my second critical leadership lesson.

In order to grow, you have to get out of your comfort zone. Sometimes you just have to make the leap, and when you do, you'll find powerful wings to take you to heights you had not imagined.

Growth and comfort do not peacefully coexist.

Chapter 4:
Took Big Risks and Failed in a Very Public Way

You're going to fail sometimes, and that's a good thing. Failure is how you learn what works and what doesn't work, what you're good at and what you need to work on, what you love and what drains you. Failure forces you to grow, it makes you stronger, smarter, bolder. A career without failure is a career played way too safely from the sidelines.

J.K. Rowling said, "It is impossible to live without failing at something, unless you live so cautiously that you might as well not have lived at all. In which case, you've failed by default."

I have experienced many failures in my career and life. Not because I was reckless or careless, but because I was willing to step out there and take some risks. And because I'm human.

I was now in my early 30s, I had advanced at a steady pace and found myself in a senior manager role as a vice president of sales and business development, with continued responsibility for customer service and new responsibility for marketing, technology development and capital spending. I was newly promoted and leading a business unit, the youngest senior manager in the company, and aside from one of our corporate attorneys I was the only female at the vice president level.

Over time I had learned to get out of my comfort zone and I had developed confidence in my own abilities and my network of relationships across the business. I was excited about taking on another new role, excited about all the knowledge and energy I could bring to this new organization and to the senior team.

A few weeks into my promotion, the President of the company asked me to develop and present my organization's five-year plan to the entire leadership of the company.

Now keep in mind, I was brand new in this senior manager role, and I hadn't even had time to develop a one-year plan, let alone a five-year plan. But I was eager, and I was so full of knowledge about what I wanted my team to achieve, what we needed to fix, how we would fix it, how we would take everything we did to the next level—I was bursting with exciting information I couldn't wait to share.

I had no idea how to create, or present, a five-year business plan. In fact, at that point in my career I had never even delivered a presentation to an audience using PowerPoint slides, never spoken in front of audience anywhere near the size this one would be. But I didn't let those little facts dampen my enthusiasm one little bit.

I thought about asking for help, but I made a mistake that I have since seen many new leaders make.

I thought, I'm at a senior level of leadership in the business, they will expect me to know how to do this. If I ask for help, they will think I was promoted too quickly, they will think I don't deserve to be in this position.

Have you ever had that thought before?

So I got busy and jumped right into the task ahead of me. I create a PowerPoint presentation that would make Tolstoy proud! I put absolutely everything I knew and wanted to achieve in that presentation. It was one of those presentations that has four to six graphs on every page and the rest of the space is filled with whole paragraphs in 10-point type.

That PowerPoint contained every detail, every contingency, every rationale, fully explored and explained. It was 45 slides long. It was awesome in my mind!

I rehearsed and practiced, focusing solely on making sure I could expertly cover all of the information contained on those slides, never paying attention to how long I was taking.

On the big day I stepped to the stage, in front of the entire leadership team and every employee in the company, over 250 people, and launched enthusiastically into my presentation.

And five minutes in, I was hit with a moment of absolute, terrifying clarity:

It's going to take me about an hour to get through this presentation at the pace I'm going.

I had twenty minutes on the agenda.

I was on the third slide, and I now had fifteen minutes to cover my remaining 42 slides.

I glanced at my boss in the front of the room hoping for a little sign of confidence. He was clearly avoiding eye contact. In fact, the entire leadership team was on the front row, and every one of them was uncomfortably glancing around and avoiding eye contact with me.

I focused on the faces around the room, looking for a few friends who might give me nods of encouragement, and saw nothing but blank stares. And a few eye rolls.

I felt sweat breaking out on my forehead, and got that queasy feeling in the pit of my stomach.

Less than ten minutes in, I already knew very clearly that I had failed, but I wasn't experienced enough to know how to get out of it gracefully. I had rehearsed with such a granular level of detail that I didn't know how to lift it up to a high level and just give the highlights on each slide so I could make it through my deck.

They say that leadership is the ability to hide your panic from others.

I was clearly not exhibiting good leadership… I was panicked and I knew they could all see it.

So I did what any self-respecting, terrified manager does in these situations: I talked faster.

And the further behind I got, the faster I talked.

Oh, and louder.

And of course, the faster and louder I talked the more I stumbled over my words, and the audience continued to shift uncomfortably in their seats, glance at their watches, and look everywhere but at me. I could see that they were embarrassed for me.

I was, at least, smart enough to know that there was no way I could stay on stage and run way over my time. So after twenty minutes, on slide 14 (of 45 mind you), I paused and said, "There is a lot more that I'd like to share with you but that's all the time I have. Thank you." And I crept off the stage, mortified.

It's painful just remembering that day, it still makes me queasy with embarrassment.

I had taken a risk by not asking for help, wanting to show everyone how much I knew, and I had failed very publicly.

But I had a choice: Stay down or get back up.

I made a decision: I was not going to let this define me. I knew that if I didn't fix this it would be the way people remembered me. I would be defined, and limited, by this failure.

We all have a tendency to keep replaying the tape in our heads after a failure. Going through it over and over again, wallowing in our failure and reliving it all over.

That's exactly what I did for the rest of that day—I replayed it over and over again in my mind, every embarrassing moment on that stage, and the more I did it the worse I felt.

I finally realized that if I continued to do that, I would grind myself up over it, lose confidence, and it would not in any way fix the problem.

Instead, I felt I had to take control, *own* the failure, and fix it.

I went straight to my boss the next morning, still feeling that sick feeling in the pit of my stomach, and the words tumbled out. I said, "I know I failed; I let you down. You put me in this position and now people are questioning whether you made the right decision. I let myself down, and I know I'm capable of doing better. I want you to know that I own this, and I will fix this. I commit to you that it will never happen again. I'm enrolling in a public speaking course and I'm determined to become a competent speaker that you can be proud of."

My boss listened with some discomfort, I could tell my poor performance was still a painful memory for him. But to my surprise he didn't re-hash it with me, he didn't beat me up over it; I believe he knew that I was beating myself up over it already and he didn't need to pile on and make me feel any worse. He told me he appreciated me stepping up to admit my poor performance before he had to call me in to address it, and he supported my plan to get it fixed. But he made it clear, it was something I had to fix.

I immediately enrolled in a public speaking course—the horrible (but effective) kind of course where you have to watch yourself on video delivering a speech. And I saw just how painful it was to listen to myself speak fast, stumble over my words, and try to cover way too much information.

The instructor taught me the fundamentals of presentation skills. He worked with me on slowing down my speech, emphasizing key points, and having an effective opening and closing. He taught me how to deliver a message with the right level of detail, tailored to the audience and the time allotted.

I dug in and I took it all in, and I grew. I learned how to create an effective PowerPoint presentation and speak in a way that the audience could relate to. I learned that you don't have to dump everything you know into a presentation—people will never know what you didn't say, *they will only remember the points you made well.*

It took a lot of painstaking work and practice, but I got better. And then a few months after my business plan presentation failure there was another opportunity to deliver a presentation to the entire employee base of the company. I went to my boss and said, "I'd like to do it; I'd like to be the one to deliver that presentation. I know I can do it—please give me a chance to demonstrate to you and others that I'm a capable leader who can deliver a message well."

I could see the concern on his face; this was an important presentation and it was critical that it be done well. He sat in silence, looking down, clearly uncomfortable with what I was asking. I watched his face as he wrestled with whether he could take this risk, take this chance on me.

I was convinced he was going to turn me down, and in my mind I was already saying, "I tried, I did my best, and at least he knows I have enough confidence in myself that I believe I could do it."

But to my surprise, he looked up and said ok. He also looked me straight in the eye and said, "I'm placing my trust in you, I'm giving you this chance, don't let me down."

There was no way I was going to let him down. This time I asked for help in creating the presentation. I made sure that the points I included were only what my colleagues agreed were the most relevant points. I created slides that were clean, crisp, and conveyed messages that could be absorbed quickly. I practiced in front of others and asked for their feedback, and I adjusted accordingly.

I was prepared...and a few weeks later I delivered that presentation in a masterful way. I nailed it. The faces that looked back at me from the audience that day were very different from what I had experienced before—they were full of pride and approval.

Henry Ford of Ford Motor Company said, "Failure is simply a way to begin again more intelligently."

I learned from my mistake, I began again much more intelligently, and I recovered from that very public failure.

And I had learned my third critical leadership lesson—

When you fail, and you *will* fail, own it, learn from it, and fix it. And then move on. Don't let it define you, and don't try to excuse it or run from it. Failures and mistakes don't get better with age.

Failures are not life sentences; they are life *lessons*. More people would learn from their mistakes if they weren't so busy replaying the tape, running from them, or denying them.

Put yourself out there, take some risks, and don't be afraid of falling down. You will learn and grow from it. Failure is not falling down—it's staying down. Be determined to get back up and try it again, armed with what you learned. I did it, I got back up and tried again and succeeded, and I know you can do it too.

Chapter 5: Took a Stand and Put My Family First

I was married when I had started with the printing company, and after my husband and I had been married for several years, and had suffered an earlier miscarriage, we were blessed with the birth of a son. I was a manager at the time, my career was advancing at a fast pace, and my responsibilities required frequent travel.

You probably can relate to the fact that it isn't easy juggling work and family. I felt the burden of being the primary bread-winner as well as the primary care-giver, and looking back now I wish I had been better prepared, and had built a stronger support network, to enable me to handle that stress. I was juggling a lot of balls every single day, and the pressure was sometimes overwhelming.

On top of that, my husband and I had different priorities when it came to work, our son, and financial concerns. Eventually our differences became unsolvable and we divorced. He left Atlanta to pursue a great career opportunity in another city, and I found myself in the position of having a demanding job and a promising career ahead of me, and raising my son by myself, with very little support close by.

A few years after we divorced, I was promoted to Vice President and General Manager and was now a member of the executive team. I was the only woman at the President's leadership table. And I was a single mom.

My son was five years old at the time, and we lived a good distance away (in Atlanta traffic) from any other member of my family. I had managed to do a fairly good job of balancing work and family up to this point, managing to get dinner on the table every night—even if it was occasionally frozen pizza and take-out.

But now I found myself faced with greater responsibility and a new set of obligations and challenges that would stretch my ability to do it all.

I was fortunate to work with a fantastic group of colleagues; these were smart, dedicated leaders with great family values. I considered these men not only colleagues, but friends.

This was the early '90s, the days of Prince, parachute pants, and *Twin Peaks*, and times were very different then, so it may be hard for you to relate completely to what it was like. Let me paint the picture for you so you can understand how challenging it was to be the only woman on the team, and a single mom.

Dual income households were still the minority in those days, and none of my colleagues' wives had a career outside of the home. It was common in those days for men to stay at the office, even if their work was done, until it was time to go home and sit down to eat with the family. It was just the way it was; and it was the routine most of my colleagues had followed for so many years.

When the workday ended, many of my colleagues dedicated some time to reading the newspaper until it was time to head home for dinner. I was typically the one running out at 5:30 so I could get my son from daycare before they closed at 6:00. As I was flying down the hall on my way to the parking garage I would pass the offices where my colleagues were catching up on the news and winding down their day.

This was a manufacturing operation that ran 24/7, and there was frequently a need to work late, or even to work an occasional night or weekend shift. For most of my male colleagues that wasn't a problem. It presented a different set of challenges for me however, and I constantly worried about how those challenges set me apart and made me different from my male colleagues. Let me share an example.

Several days a week the President held a meeting of his leadership team at 4 p.m. so we could review the day's operations and plan for the work that would occur on the second and third shifts that night. The meeting was scheduled for an hour every day, scheduled to end at 5 p.m.

I was the only one around that table who cared if that meeting ended on time. Because I was a single mother with a child in daycare and no family close by, and the daycare closed at 6 p.m.

Several days a week that meeting ran long and no one else around that table was at all concerned about it. But every day that the meeting was still going at 5:15 and the team just kept talking, I began to squirm and to sweat.

I knew I had to leave that room by 5:30 to get to the daycare before they closed. No one else at that table had that challenge, or in fairness, even really thought about it or understood it.

There were no cell phones or devices in those days. I couldn't pull out my smartphone and discreetly text someone under the table while I continued to participate in the meeting. The word "texting" didn't even exist then.

So every day I sat in that meeting, watching as the clock ticked toward 5:30, squirming as I wrestled with the choices in my head—

Do I leave the room now and scramble to make calls to find someone who can pick up my son before 6:00—calling attention to myself, disrupting the meeting, and making it obvious that I was the "different" one in the group?

Do I sit tight and hope the meeting ends by 5:30 and hope I can make it?

Or do I just stay in the meeting as long as I can and then run out before it ends to race to get my son?

None of those were elegant choices. And every one of them would be disruptive, making me stand out as not like the others.

It was incredibly stressful. And too many days I was the last one at the daycare center to pick up their child. Too many days I arrived to find my son sitting on the front steps with the daycare owner. And I realized that wasn't going to work, I couldn't continue to do that to my son.

So I took a risk—I set up a meeting to talk with my boss about it.

I said, "You know how committed I am, you know I work hard, and you know that over the years I have demonstrated that I will do what it takes to get the job done and drive this business forward. But every day when our production meeting runs long I'm faced with the problem of how to get my son from daycare before they close."

And I asked for his help.

I said, "I'm always willing to stay late if necessary, but I need some advance notice on when the meeting will run long so I have time to line up care for my son before the meeting begins. That way I can stay in the room and participate until it ends."

I also pointed out that on some days the meeting seemed to run long just because people felt comfortable staying and chatting, and I suggested that if he officially wrapped it up it would allow me to leave gracefully and not look like I was running out like a crazy person.

We had a very healthy conversation about the challenges I was wrestling with and he was very understanding. He acknowledged that it just hadn't occurred to him what I might be dealing with as a single mom in a demanding leadership position. He understood my predicament, and he committed to trying to be more conscious of time in those afternoon meetings and to offer his support and help where he could.

I asked for one more trade-off. I said, "There is occasionally a need for someone to come in on the weekends, and I'd rather do all of the late duty during the week so that I can have my weekends with my son." I spent enough time away from him during the week and I wanted Saturdays and Sundays free to dedicate time to him.

Looking back at that conversation, I think it's important to note that I didn't just present him with a problem and ask him to solve it.

I presented him with solutions and options. I gave him something he could work with.

He made it a point from then on to end the meetings on time. Rarely did the meeting ever run past 5:15. He would bring the meeting to a close and suggest that if anyone wanted to stay and talk longer, they could come by his office. He managed it so I didn't feel singled out as being different from the rest of the group.

And I learned my fourth critical leadership lesson—

There are always tradeoffs that have to be made, but stay grounded in your values, set boundaries when you need to, and make time for the things that are important to you. When the stress of having too much on your plate becomes unmanageable, as mine did when my increased responsibilities were taking too much time away from my son, sit down and think through options and then take action and ask for help.

All of us, every day, are juggling a lot of balls at the same time. But we need to understand that some of those balls are rubber balls, and some are crystal. If you drop a rubber ball, it will bounce, maybe someone else will pick it up as it bounces, maybe it will bounce until you can get back to it again.

But the crystal balls don't bounce—if you drop a crystal ball it shatters, and you can never put it back together again. It is forever lost.

Know which balls are your crystal balls, and make sure you always put those first in your life.

Another example of stepping up to set boundaries and making leaders aware of the work/life integration challenges they were inadvertently creating for their people occurred much later in my career.

Many years later, I was a seasoned Senior Vice President working with a peer team of outstanding, smart, genuine, caring senior leaders. They were all tremendous drivers of results. They worked their people hard and the work involved long hours, but they all understood the need for balance and tried hard to ensure they were respectful of the challenges people faced when juggling work and life.

One day we were all together in a meeting with our boss, and we were going through a "Speed of Trust" exercise, focused on Stephen M.R. Covey's 13 Behaviors of High Trust Leaders. The conversation evolved to a discussion of whether we were creating the right environment and demonstrating the right behaviors by not driving our people to respond to emails at nights and on weekends.

Each of my peers spoke up and said they were very conscious of the fact that as senior leaders we tend to work all the time, and they each described how they avoided having their people feel that they needed to keep up the same work schedule as their leader.

Now I was aware that these leaders, with all the best intentions, were doing some things that were in fact causing their people to have to work on the weekends and always be connected and checking email. And I knew I had to work up the courage to constructively help them understand.

Our boss said, "I only send emails to people on the weekends at 8 a.m. Saturday morning. That's when I look back over the week and write all my emails recognizing great work and thanking people for their contributions. And those don't require anyone to work over the weekend, I don't expect a response."

I said, "With all due respect, let me describe how that plays out with our people.

"A manager gets up on a Saturday morning, she bundles her family into the car and they head out to the soccer fields for the day. She leaves her device at home, knowing that there is no work she has to address today and this is her quality time with her family. She gets home that afternoon after a great day with her family, she looks at her device, and she realizes she received an email at 8 a.m. that morning from the big boss. She has a moment of sheer panic. She received an email from the big boss eight hours ago and never responded. She reads the email and realizes it's a thank you email, but she still feels that letting eight hours pass without acknowledging it sent the wrong signal—that she was disconnected and not available should the boss have really been trying to reach her.

"So she responds to the boss's email to acknowledge his feedback. But from that day forward she will likely never leave her device at home, and will regularly check at night and on weekends to see if there are emails she should respond to."

I pointed out that even innocent emails of appreciation on a Saturday morning can cause employees to feel that they must have their device with them and be checking email all the time.

There were some looks of surprise around the room as everyone realized the impact we, as leaders, can inadvertently have on our people, even with the best of intentions.

Then another leader proudly said, "I don't send any emails on the weekend. I do work all weekend, I have to in order to keep up, but I save all my emails and schedule them to be delivered to people first thing Monday morning so they don't have to respond on the weekend."

I said, "That is also having an unintended impact on our people.

"Every Monday morning, they come in with their day planned, they have a packed agenda and a list of things they need to get done in addition to all the needs that typically arise during the day. They get to work, already daunted by the full day of work ahead of them. And then your emails pop in, and it is typically not just one or two informational emails, it's often many emails that require investigation, analysis, and meetings in order to respond with what you asked for. Their entire day just got disrupted, and now they face a Monday with more work than they can possibly complete.

"Over time, your people realize that they *have* to work over the weekend to get ahead of their own to-do list so that they have time to handle all the emails that pop in Monday morning. In fact, they would *prefer* that you just send your emails over the weekend so they can get them handled and out of the way in preparation for their own Monday workload."

The leaders in that meeting all understood, and maybe it didn't happen overnight, but bit by bit, we learned not to be tethered to our emails. To their credit, they all became more mindful of the impact of their actions on the work/life challenges of their people.

To this day, one of those leaders credits that conversation with not only changing the lives of his people, but changing his own life as well. He says he learned to stop working over the weekend, and he got a little bit of his own personal life back in the process.

So integrating work and life is difficult. It requires a conscious focus -leaders have to be diligent about understanding how their own behavior is causing their people to struggle, and employees need to have the courage to give constructive feedback, ask for help, and offer solutions that enable more effective work/life integration.

Make sure you know which of the balls you are juggling are made of crystal, and never let those drop. For me, it was my family, and I took a stand and put my family first.

Chapter 6:
Leadership Lessons They Don't Teach You in Business School

There are fundamental leadership capabilities and competencies that are consistently taught and written about that are critical to being a successful leader. Integrity, delegation, decisiveness, accountability, empathy, communication, listening, focus. Much has been written about these leadership characteristics and you just have to do a Google search to learn about them. They have been well covered by others, so those aren't the capabilities I'm going to talk about here.

Instead, I'd like to share a few of the subtler lessons I've learned over time, through my experiences. Insights I wish someone had been able to share with me early in my career.

I call these *leadership lessons they don't teach you in business school,* and I think they are the characteristics that truly distinguish good leaders from great leaders.

Find the White Space, Where You Can Make a Unique Difference

I have mentored hundreds of people over the years, and I have spoken to many groups of people about leadership and career development and advancement.

One of the questions I am most often asked is "What do you look for in leaders, what are the qualities and characteristics that cause you to select one person over another for a promotion?"

One of my most common answers is—I look for people who don't just manage the status quo, but who nail their job and then look for the white space that no one else is addressing, and they find a way to fill it.

Let's go back to one of my first examples of the keys to my early success—Make Great Coffee.

The primary lesson from that example was: do whatever is asked of you and do it better than anyone else.

But there is a secondary lesson in that example that is equally important. As I look back on that time, I realize that because my role as a clerk wasn't fully defined, I had to look for my own ways to add value. And in hindsight, what I did was find the white space.

Because I was connecting with so many different managers and I was asking them to share with me what they did and who they interacted with, I was in a unique position to see the white space, or the gaps that existed between departments and functions. I saw the areas where a process change could eliminate duplication and work, I saw the details and instructions that were being missed when work was being passed from team to team, and I heard the complaints managers raised about things that got in their way.

And I fixed them—I suggested process changes, I tightened up instruction forms, I streamlined reports, I brought to light the issues and concerns managers didn't feel comfortable raising. It wasn't in my job description, but I saw opportunities that weren't being addressed by anyone else and I knew I could make a difference.

I developed a reputation right then, in that role as a clerk, for being someone who will always do whatever is asked of them and nail my job, and then will look around and find the white space and fill it.

That's one of the reasons I was asked to take over the sales organization—because I had shored up my own customer service organization, I got my own house in order, and then I had reached out to address the gaps that existed between customer service and sales. In the process of doing that, I addressed opportunities that helped the sales organization function more effectively as well.

So when people ask me what I look for when it's time to promote someone, that's the leader I look for.

Not the worker who just keeps his head down, focused on doing only his job while trying to stay off the radar screen and not make waves.

Not the worker who is so worried about his own success and next opportunity that he is more likely to elbow other leaders out of the way than to help the whole team succeed.

Not the worker who, when asked to help with a project or task, says "not my job."

I look for the worker who nails his job and then finds the white space, determined to make a difference by addressing the things that no one else is addressing. The leader who reaches out to help other team members before they even ask for assistance. The leader who, not coincidentally, is most likely to emerge as a natural leader among his peers.

Confidence Trumps Brilliance—Silence Your Inner Critic and Find Your Voice

In their book *The Confidence Code,* Katty Kay and Claire Shipman write about the importance of confidence and the surprising fact that even highly successful women suffer from nagging self-doubt. They interviewed some of the most successful women in a variety of professions—lawmakers and CEOs, professional athletes, leaders of social movements. They repeatedly saw the same trend: smart, influential women with great credentials and track records who have the inexplicable feeling that their position is tenuous, that they don't actually deserve to be at the top.

Sheryl Sandberg, in her book *Lean In,* talks about the "imposter effect," which afflicts women who, "despite being high achievers, even experts in their fields ... can't seem to shake the sense that it is only a matter of time until they are found out for who they really are—imposters with limited skills or abilities." It's astonishing that this is a feeling that even someone as accomplished as Sandberg has experienced. But the reality is, it affects both men and women, and can be a serious obstacle to us achieving our potential.

Women do tend to be harder on themselves than men are, often believing that they're surrounded by people who are smarter than them, who are more deserving of a seat at the table. When something at work goes wrong, women are more likely to blame themselves, to replay the tape in their head and beat themselves up over their personal failure. When something goes right, they tend to credit circumstance, luck, or other people for their success. Men tend to do the opposite.

Studies have shown that women apply for a promotion only when they believe they meet close to 100 percent of the qualifications, believing that they must be perfectly prepared to excel when they step into a new role. Men apply when they meet 50 percent, assuming they will learn and grow into the job. When women are asked to step up to a new role or take on additional responsibility they often ask, "Do you think I'm ready?" Men more often ask, "How high, how fast, when do I start?"

Women lack confidence, and it can be a stumbling block to success. I have experienced that self-doubt many times in my career, allowing my inner critic to convince me that I'm not good enough, that I don't belong. That lack of confidence can prevent us from pursuing stretch roles and assignments. It can keep us from building a powerful network with well-positioned mentors and sponsors. And it can keep us from speaking up and having a voice at the table.

When the printing company I worked for was acquired by BellSouth, I had an opportunity to learn first-hand how important it is to silence your inner critic, find your voice and be a confident, active participant in any group or meeting.

In the mid '90s I had the chance to move out of the printing company and step into a big new role in BellSouth as the VP of Publishing. I had spent 15 years in the printing business, and I found myself for the first time in my career in a business I didn't know, sitting at a leadership table with other senior leaders that I hadn't "grown up with." I was no longer the subject matter expert in the business, and that was a big change and a new experience for me.

As I stepped in to this new role I let my newness to the team, my lack of knowledge of that business, and lack of familiarity with my new peers shake my confidence. Sitting in meetings with this talented group of professionals and listening to them discuss the business they knew inside and out only increased my discomfort at how much I had to learn and how little I felt I was able to contribute. I began to question whether I even deserved to be at that table.

I became uncharacteristically quiet, observing the conversation around me but not participating. There were times when I had a question in my head that I wanted to ask, or an idea that I thought might have merit, but I didn't have the confidence to speak up. I thought, I can't possibly have a better idea than all of these experienced managers, they are all much smarter than me. I was afraid that if I spoke up they would all see that I was an imposter who didn't have the credentials to be there.

That lack of confidence can strike us over and over again, can paralyze us, even when we have years of proven success under our belts.

I had been in this new role only a few weeks when one day I was walking down the hall, passing the office of one of my peers, and I saw several of them huddled together having what looked like a serious conversation about the business. I wondered for a moment why they hadn't included me. The next day I heard about a decision that had been made in that meeting that affected my team in a minor way, and I wondered why my input hadn't been sought.

It all of a sudden hit me—the alarming realization that I wasn't seen as being an important part of the conversation. Because I wasn't actively participating in the dialogue at the table, my peers didn't think about including me in other discussions that were happening outside of these meetings. They didn't see me as an essential team member and decision-maker.

I realized that my reputation and my effectiveness were at stake. The longer I sat there as a silent observer without speaking up, the more I looked like I had nothing to contribute, that I didn't bring anything of value to the table, and the more I would be excluded from important discussions and decisions. I realized I had to find my voice quickly and become part of the conversation.

I made up my mind at that moment that I would not sit through another meeting without participating. So I did my homework, I studied, and I prepared. I wrote down a list of questions that had been rolling around in my head but I hadn't found the courage to ask. I met with a few of my peers to get some insight on what they planned to present in the next meeting, and then I spent time thinking through my views on the topic and the impact it might have on my organization. I talked with some of my key managers to get their input on items or issues they thought I needed to raise in the meeting.

When the meeting rolled around I was nervous, but I was ready. Within the first 10 minutes of the meeting I jumped in and asked my first question. My confidence was buoyed when the others around the table raised their eyebrows with interest, welcoming my question and participation. I noticed that the more I joined the dialogue, the more others turned to me and sought my input. Several times a question I asked resulted in a spirited debate and at one point even a change in direction. And I pushed back on decisions that would negatively impact my team, and watched my peers sit up and take notice, appreciating my courage in standing up for my team.

I was an active participant in that meeting, and my peers noticed. I didn't just join the conversation, I *added to the content and direction of that meeting.* I had prepared, and I found my voice that day. As the meeting came to a close, I realized that I never should have let my inner critic derail my confidence—I had the knowledge and the credentials all along, and the right to be at that table.

You don't need to look for acceptance or validation from others. You know what you're capable of doing, you are smart, knowledgeable, and prepared—be confident enough to *assume* your right to be at the table.

What I learned from my experience was that your input, idea, or question doesn't have to be brilliant. What matters is confidence. The people who are actively engaged and part of the dialogue, who are leaning forward, who speak with confidence and conviction, are viewed as competent and knowledgeable. Their confidence gives them credibility, and they are consistently perceived as the individuals who are the most engaged, the strongest contributors, and even the most intelligent.

At the end of a meeting, no one remembers the people who sat there as silent observers—they aren't the ones who stand out in anyone's mind. What you remember are the people who talked, asked questions, and engaged. You remember them as the thought leaders, the drivers, and the influencers.

A striking example of how confidence, or lack of it, affects credibility occurred while I was in that same position at BellSouth. One of the women around the table was an experienced leader, known as someone who was reliable and a go-to person but not really considered a thought leader in the business. I observed, more than once, that she would put an idea on the table or draw a conclusion from the dialogue taking place that was insightful. She didn't speak with a lot of confidence, but I always thought her input was right on target. The others, however, would often move past it and not really acknowledge it. Minutes later, one of our male colleagues would put the same idea or conclusion on the table, phrased a little differently, and everyone would unanimously concur that it was brilliant and accurate. I'm not saying the man intentionally hijacked her idea, it's just that he presented it with the *confidence* and conviction to make everyone around the table take notice and pay attention.

You don't want that to be you. Take up your space at the table, lean forward, and speak with confidence and conviction. The first time someone walks over you, take the floor back and state your point again. When someone restates your idea and others treat it like a new idea, use humor to point out how masterfully they repositioned what you just said.

We spend years developing and honing our *competence*, but we don't spend as much time working on our confidence. Yet confidence is every bit as important as competence. Develop and hone your confidence—it is critical to your success.

The simplest and most basic questions, asked with confidence, sound intelligent. Confidently emphasizing or reframing a point a colleague previously made comes across as engaged and insightful. Putting a new idea on the table, challenging a previously made decision, or drawing a conclusion from the discussion, and doing it with confidence, is perceived as strong and decisive leadership.

Those who speak up in a timid or insecure way are often overlooked or ignored, even if their input is intelligent and on the mark. And those who don't speak up at all eventually become invisible.

Confidence can make or break the way you are perceived. Speak up, do it with confidence, and be a part of the conversation.

This is a lesson I had to learn, and one that I had to constantly work on throughout my career. You see, I'm one of those people who doesn't like to repeat or rehash what others have said. I dislike redundancy and consider it a time drain. I don't like to restate the obvious. I don't like to pile on when I feel a point has already been well made. And I don't like to slow the group down with a question that might derail the conversation.

I'm a fan of crisp, short meetings with appropriate discussion and debate, but to then decide and move on so we can go drive action.

But I realized that with that attitude I could, and in some cases had, become invisible. And leaders who are invisible have no influence. I knew that I would have to work at it, but that being an active and confident participant in every dialogue was critical to my ability to be seen as relevant and influential.

One other observation I've made is that men and women approach asking questions in meetings in very different ways. I'll use an example to explain it.

I was speaking at a Multi-Cultural Diversity Conference at a major university. The audience was a couple hundred graduate and undergraduate students. I gave a talk on what these diverse students could expect as they entered the corporate world, and how important is was that they understood and appreciated the unique value they would bring to so many companies who are seeking diversity of thought, background, experience, cultures, gender, and education in the workforce.

When I finished my presentation I opened it up for questions. About 20 minutes into the Q&A, a young woman close to the back of the room raised her hand and asked a question. She said, "I'm a biochemical engineer and am currently doing an internship with a large engineering firm. In this field I often find myself in an environment that is all men. How do you develop the confidence to participate and ask questions when you're the only female, when you're different from everyone else?" Such a great question.

I first said to her, "Let me ask you a question. How long did you sit there and formulate that question in your head before you were willing to ask it? Did you silently practice it over and over again and keep rephrasing it to ensure it was going to sound intelligent?"

She sheepishly said yes, that she had been trying to get the nerve to ask her question since I opened it up for Q&A, and she had rehearsed it over and over again in her head.

I then turned to several of the young men in the room who had already asked their questions. I asked them how many times they had rephrased the question over and over in their head before they asked it.

Blank stares. None of them rehearsed a question—they thought of a question and they just shot their hand up and eagerly hoped I'd call on them. None of them worried about whether their question would seem dumb.

This young woman was a biochemical engineer, she was brilliant, poised, articulate, professional, and she was fearful of asking a question that made her sound dumb.

Why do we do that to ourselves—nervously and silently rehearse a question and wait so long to ask it, even as we listen to those around us ask questions that we know aren't particularly brilliant?

At least she did eventually ask her question. What about all those others who didn't?

My advice to myself, and to you, is that you need to set a goal that you hold yourself accountable to. In any meeting that is an hour long, you should ask at least two questions and weigh in on at least one dialogue or debate. Even if it is restating or reframing what someone else said, you need to find your voice and participate, with confidence. Prepare in advance if you need to. But don't let the opportunity pass.

For a presentation-style meeting with a speaker or senior leader, you don't have to be the one to ask a question in every meeting, but make up your mind that you're *not* going to sit quietly in the audience every single time, avoiding eye contact so you don't get called on. Be prepared with a question and ask it with confidence.

Trust me—I've seen it play out over and over again. Confidence trumps brilliance. Get over your fear of asking a dumb question or making a foolish comment—it's just not going to happen. If you prepare, if you speak up and do it confidently you will be perceived as intelligent, engaged, and motivated. You will be remembered as being a valuable participant. And that matters.

Respect Everyone – You Never Know Who Will Influence Your Career

Over the course of my career, I've seen too many leaders who are smart, strategic, and drivers of results, but who fail to lead people in the right way. These leaders seem to believe that the only thing that matters is whether you get results, not *how* you get them. They only care about how those above them in the org chart see them, and ignore the importance of how their peers, subordinates, and others feel about them as a leader and a team player.

I want you to know it matters *how* you get results, how you lead people, how you treat others.

Some leaders are often referred to as "level-conscious"—the leaders who "work up," who are more focused on impressing or pleasing those above them than on caring for the people who depend on them for leadership and coaching. I've worked with leaders like this who don't even know the names of the people who work for them.

I was visiting one of my offices on the west coast at one point, meeting the director there for the first time. Roger was new to my organization, he had been in place almost four months, He had been recommended to me by his former boss who told me Roger was a strong leader and a top performer. I took that recommendation at face value and selected Roger for this critical position—he was now leading one of my teams that was not performing well and I needed someone who could improve their performance quickly. So I was anxious to meet Roger and see how he was positioning himself to turn this team around.

As I met with Roger that day, I began to wonder just how engaged he really was with his team. First of all, he seemed to barely know his way around the office. Granted it was a three story building and there were other groups in the building, and he had teams and meeting space and training rooms on multiple floors, but after four months I was surprised that he would still be struggling to remember how to get to various places in the building. At one point he actually had to ask one of his managers to show us where the training room was. It made me wonder how much time he was really spending time in the office, walking around, being visible and interacting with his people.

Then as we walked around, he didn't seem to be entirely sure of the kind of work each of his groups did. When I asked him where the team was that handled services for our military veterans, he couldn't answer, and had to ask one of the managers who reported to him.

As I stopped to talk with people as I always like to do, it was obvious that he didn't know the names of all of his managers and coaches. And when he introduced me to his very top performing coach, the coach who had won an award trip for her outstanding performance, he called her by the wrong name. I happened to know her, I had met her on that award trip, so I politely used her name a few times to give Roger the hint, but he continued to call her by the wrong name. As we walked away she just rolled her eyes and said, "It happens all the time." I was embarrassed for Roger, but he didn't appear bothered by it at all.

As we visited with various teams around the office that day, I couldn't help noticing that Roger was spending more time telling me about himself and what he was looking for in his next job than engaging with the people we were there to see. In fact, halfway through the day he asked if he could set up a separate meeting with me to discuss his next career move. I pointed out that he had only been there four months and had good deal of work to do in his current role before he thought about his next one.

I asked him to give me his observations thus far as to whether he had the right talent on his team and what steps he would take in the next 30 to 60 days to begin to improve results. He skirted around the question, talking instead about his former role and describing at length all he did to turn that team around and deliver exceptional results. His stories were all about what he did, giving his team none of the credit. He seemed focused only on trying to impress me with tales of what he had done in the past rather than talking in any level of detail about how to improve the performance of his current team.

When I left Roger's office that evening I was alarmed at the lack of engagement and substance I had seen, so the next day

I reached out to talk with others who had worked with him in the past. I talked to his former peers, who were tactful and said he was a great guy, but when I pressed they couldn't describe any unique contributions he had brought to the role or even any specific results he had personally contributed to. I talked to two of the managers who had worked for him in the past, and again they were tactful and said he was a really nice guy but they didn't see him all that much, and then they raved about their new boss who had replaced Roger—what a smart and engaged leader he was, how much he had done to remove some lingering obstacles and help the team take their performance to the next level.

I thought back to the conversation I had had with Roger's former boss who recommended him and how different his perception was, and I realized that Roger was one of those leaders who works up—he talked a good game, and had apparently done a great job of convincing his boss of how terrific he was—while his team rarely saw him and he wasn't engaged enough to be driving results or even to be seen as a strong contributor by his peers.

These "level-conscious" leaders like Roger never really engage with the teams they lead. They save their engagement for the people who really matter to them, the leaders above them, the ones they perceive can positively impact their career.

Can you imagine what it feels like to work for a leader who you don't ever see, or who can't remember your name, or who is too busy working the system to get in the trenches with the team? Or a leader who only shows their "good" side to those above them while their team constantly feels the brunt of their anger and fury, or at best their lack of leadership?

In my experience, these leaders are not only showing a lack of respect for the people they lead, they are making a grave mistake in discounting the impact that others can (and probably will) have on their career.

Roger was given feedback on expectations, and coaching on how to engage and improve performance, but his response was to double down on his efforts to find another role rather than dig in and make a difference in his current role. Unfortunately, by this time his reputation for spending more time working his boss than working his job was widely known, and he eventually left the business.

You need to be aware that the people you're interacting with on a daily basis, and how you treat them, can influence your reputation and your opportunities. Because they *will* tell others about the kind of leader you are.

I've seen examples where secretaries and assistants have impacted the careers, positively or negatively, of leaders by giving their boss the inside scoop on how a candidate treats others. How you treat an assistant, or a waiter, or a driver, is an indication of how you value others and what kind of leader you are. I've known hiring managers who, after an interview, will seek input from the staff the candidate interacted with and will refuse to hire a candidate who has treated anyone with a lack of respect.

As I've given career advice over the years, I've often said that if you are seeking advancement, you need to be the kind of leader who you would want to work for. The kind of leader who is admired and respected by your team and your peers, not just by those above you. The kind of leader that your peers and your team actually want to see promoted. That is the kind of leader who gets promoted, and continues to rise through the organization.

Putting all your energy into getting noticed by someone above you while you ignore those beside or below you is not going to get you to the top of an organization. If you're lucky, it might get you promoted once, but it isn't going to result in success over the long haul. Your progression will stall as your reputation for putting your needs ahead of others, for not respecting others, becomes known.

I learned an early lesson about respect when I joined the printing company at the start of my career. There was a gentleman who was in a position of leadership and had been with the company almost forty years. Forty years! Who can even imagine being with the same company for that long today?

I got to know this gentleman, Buster, by delivering his coffee in the morning and spending time listening to his story. He was absolutely fascinating, he had seen so much and done so much for the business, he was full of wise, sage advice and I just soaked up all of his wisdom and insights. He also had some great stories—like the time a bear somehow got into the plant and was found wandering among the large rolls of paper in the warehouse in the middle of the night. I couldn't get enough of all of *life* Buster had to share.

Not everyone at the company was as fascinated by Buster. There were people who couldn't imagine that someone who had been there 40 years could possibly be relevant, could possibly be knowledgeable about the technology or even the work today. They didn't see him for the treasured resource that he was.

But to me he was a tremendous wealth of knowledge, and over the years we became very good friends. In fact, he is in his 80s now and still active on boards and in his church and community. I was blessed to have a chance to talk with him not too long ago, and after all these years he still regaled me with stories of his adventures and his work.

Turns out that Buster played a major role in my career that I wasn't even aware of at the time.

I've already described some of my early career, and the rapid progression to management and then upper management. At the time I never really thought about how it was that I was being given so many incredible opportunities. I was just focused on digging in and learning, growing and delivering. But many years later, as I reflected on that time in my career, I realized that I didn't even know the word "sponsor" at the time, but Buster was my sponsor.

You never know who might be in a position to be your sponsor.

In reminiscing with Buster about those times, he told me that every time a position was open he would sit with the President and the leadership team and say, "Give Debbie a chance." "Debbie can do that job." "Debbie is perfect for that role."

He wasn't successful the first time he tried, or the second, or perhaps even the tenth time, but eventually the leaders listened, and they took notice of the work I was doing and the reputation I had earned. And one of those times that Buster said "Give Debbie a chance" they said ok.

I've always reflected on this as a lesson in respect. Respect is not the same thing as brown-nosing. Respect has to be genuine for it to matter.

I didn't show such admiration and respect for Buster because I thought he could do something for me. I genuinely regarded him as an individual with a rich history and story, someone I could learn from. And as he got to know me and my abilities he became my sponsor.

Those people you dismiss as not being important enough to spend your time on might one day be in a position to help you get your next big opportunity.

Those employees on your team whose names you haven't taken the time to know—they'll tell others you're a leader who doesn't engage, and who doesn't care about their people.

Those colleagues you respect, help, and support along the way will tell others you're a leader everyone wants to work for, a leader people would walk through walls for, a leader people want to follow.

Every single person you meet along the way is a person with a history and a story, a person who is relevant, who is worthy of your respect. Treat everyone with respect because it's the right thing to do. And remember—you never know who will have the ability to affect your career.

Communicate Frequently, Openly, and Honestly, and Make It a Two-Way Dialogue

Never underestimate the importance of open, honest, and frequent communication. It is often thought of as the most important leadership trait, because without it, it is nearly impossible to become a great leader.

Take a look at the world's greatest leaders, whether in business, politics, sports, or the military. The best leaders are strong communicators. Their values are clear and solid, and their words convey those values. They say what they mean and do what they say. They listen, adjust, and take the time to ensure their message is taking root. Their teams trust them, admire them and willingly follow them.

I learned the value of honest, direct communication when I first joined BellSouth. As I stepped into my new role, I was told that a decision had just been made to decentralize one of the functions within my organization.

The art department consisted of about 350 artists all in Atlanta, and after much studying, testing, and deliberating, the decision had been made to place all of those jobs out into the field so that artists could be co-located with sales and closer to the customer.

That decision made sense to me. I understood enough about the business to know that having sales people and artists working more closely together would improve communication and collaboration, shorten turnaround times, reduce errors, and contribute to a tighter relationship with the customer.

The artists had not yet been told that their jobs would be affected, and one of my first duties in my new role was to host a meeting of all of the artists in Atlanta, then the entire team, and inform them about this change.

As my HR team was preparing me for the meeting, they said to me, "Look, you're new in this role so all we really want you to do is open the meeting, tell them that the work is being decentralized and their jobs will be moving out in the field throughout the nine southeast states, and then turn it over to us and we'll go through all the details with them."

With all due respect to my HR partners who were just trying to help me manage a tough situation in my new role, I was appalled. I said, "Absolutely not. This is my team, and I'm responsible for their work *and* their well-being. This change will have a *huge* impact on their lives. I owe it to them to stand with them, to spend the time explaining the rationale for the change, and to let them ask all the questions they want. I'll spend as long as I need to with them to help them absorb this change."

So I stood in front of the group and introduced myself as their new leader. I spent a good bit of time giving them the background on this decision and walking them through the rationale so they could understand the business reasons for the change. I told them that there would be opportunities for many of them to follow their work in the field, and that many of them would be able to remain in their roles in Atlanta. But I acknowledged that some of them would be faced with the loss of their jobs.

I didn't want to sugar coat it, I had enough respect for them and how this change impacted them to just tell them the unvarnished truth.

But I said one more thing to this group of 350 people. I said, "I commit to you that I personally will be involved, and that we will help every one of you walk through your options with the goal of finding as many of you a job as we can, even if it is in another part of the company."

And then, against the advice of my HR partners, I opened it up for questions. They told me I would be slaughtered if I allowed questions, that their anger would be directed at me.

I didn't care; it was the right thing to do. I had just told 350 people about a massive change that was completely out of their control. I had told them there would be a period of uncertainty as we worked to place people in roles and helped some to relocate and follow their work. And I had just acknowledged that some people would find themselves without a job.

I owed it to them to let them vent.

I spent the next hour taking questions. There was a lot of anger, a lot of concern, and a lot of just great questions. I stayed with them until there were no more hands raised.

And then I thanked them. I told them they had just experienced one of the toughest things that can happen to an individual during their career, and that I understood how devastating this decision must be to them. I thanked them for bearing with me, working with me, and getting all the questions on the table. I thanked them for sharing their anxiety and concerns with me. And I reiterated my promise to personally work with them to see this through to the best possible outcome for each and every one of them.

As I ended the meeting I let them know my door was open to anyone who wanted to spend more time talking through the change.

I earned their trust and their respect that day. They certainly didn't all leave the meeting feeling good, that wasn't even possible.

But they left feeling that they had a leader at the helm who would always be honest, shoot straight, communicate the full story, and support them with genuine care and concern.

Many leaders make the mistake of thinking it's better not to give people bad news.

Many leaders underestimate people's need to have the full story, the background and context of a decision, in order to process it properly.

People don't fear bad news...they fear the unknown.

People don't fear change...they fear the loss of control.

Great leaders have enough respect and trust for their people to be willing to take the time to give them all the information, context, choices, and options they need to understand that reason for a change, accept it, and process the implications to them.

Great leaders don't just dump a message on a team and go back to their office. They enable a two-way dialogue to ensure questions are answered, concerns are addressed, and they truly listen and take into account the feedback.

Then great leaders help people focus on the things they *can* control.

Open, honest communication creates trust. When a team trusts that a leader will communicate the full story, they don't get distracted by searching for the truth, reading between the lines, and using conjecture to piece together their own version of the truth.

Always communicate openly, honestly, and authentically to your team.

Relationships Matter

I told the story earlier of how Buster taught me the value of showing respect for everyone. He became not only a sponsor and good friend, but a role model who shaped the way I led throughout my entire career.

There is another lesson I learned from Buster, and that is that relationships matter, they are key to getting things done and making things happen. I'm not talking about a long list of names in your contacts folder, many of whom you don't even know. I'm talking about a carefully developed and cultivated portfolio of relationships, people you can call on when you need information, action, or just help.

Buster was the primary sales contact for our largest and most important customer. He was responsible for managing the relationship between my company and BellSouth. He was ultimately responsible for every aspect of that account, and he was masterful in the way he managed relationships to ensure success.

In his role, Buster interacted with every level of leader and manager at BellSouth—from the President all the way down to the drivers who drove packages back and forth between our offices. He was genuine in the relationships he formed with them, getting to know them on a business level as well as a personal level. Every one of the people in Buster's circle of connections knew that if they needed anything, they could always count on him. And Buster was amazingly consistent in the way he dealt with people, treating everyone at all levels with the same respect and genuine interest as he did those in the very upper ranks of the company.

At this point in his career, Buster didn't have a lot of direct oversight or interaction with our internal manufacturing operations. He spent most of his time with the customer—understanding their strategic priorities and plans, listening to their thoughts on emerging technology, uncovering their concerns, and generally making himself an invaluable resource and partner for the customer.

In a large-scale manufacturing operation, things go wrong. In our directory printing operation errors occasionally happened, and when they did, they could be very costly for us or for the customer. Major errors were often very technical and weren't easy to fix, requiring quick action, intense technical troubleshooting, and difficult decisions.

Given Buster's role at this point in his career, and as the relationship manager with the customer, you might assume that he would not be the first person called when a major error was detected and quick troubleshooting was required.

But Buster was, in fact, the first person anyone called. Because he had such incredible connections and relationships that he was able to make things happen and get things done in a way that no one else could.

If we didn't have an immediate answer for something and weren't sure where to get it, Buster knew who to call, no matter what hour of the day or night. People would gladly rally and jump into action when he called. Even supervisors on the manufacturing floor would drive in to the plant, in the middle of the night, to help troubleshoot when they got the call from Buster.

If we needed the customer to be a part of the solution or help us share the cost of fixing an error, Buster could make that call and negotiate with the customer in an amazing way to make it happen.

Buster's greatest value was in the trusting relationships he had established over the years. He was always one phone call away from a solution, and people would do absolutely anything for him when he called to ask for help.

Buster had often asked me to accompany him on visits to meet with customers, and he occasionally invited me to lunches and dinners with customers and vendor partners. Many of these visits had no purpose other than to strengthen the relationship and get to know someone a little bit better. I have to admit that I wasn't always sure I saw the value of all that time spent on lunches and dinners and meetings just to develop relationships with people. I saw it as a bit of a drain on my time and I didn't spend nearly enough time nurturing relationships on my own.

But watching Buster in action taught me that time spent building strong, collaborative relationships is never a waste of time—it pays huge dividends and is absolutely critical to success.

Relationships Matter.

Build trusted, long-lasting relationships. It's hard work, but no one ever achieved lasting success without the help and support of others.

Ask Great Questions

Never underestimate the value of being able to ask great questions.

When I moved to BellSouth and stepped into my new VP role, I was thrilled and honored to be asked to step into such a significant role, but remember I was moving into a position over a business unit that I had no experience in and knew very little about.

Until that time, I had been in one business—printing—and had the luxury of learning it from the ground up. I was knowledgeable about every aspect of our operation, a recognized subject matter expert on almost every part of the business. Now I had to learn how to lead people in a business where I was no longer a subject matter expert, and it wasn't an easy transition for me.

As I was getting up to speed in my new role, I learned that we were in the middle of a huge systems transformation. The entire publishing system that ran the business—the backbone of the business that contained every bit of data on names, addresses, and telephone numbers for the entire country—was being sunset and a new system had been selected to replace it.

My team was faced with the task of managing that conversion—converting all of our data over to the new system, which had a totally different data architecture and operating system than the existing system. There were a huge number of decisions that had to be made and managed to ensure the data converted properly and the system functioned as we needed it to.

We didn't have the luxury of time in this transition, we were up against the Y2K deadline (who remembers that?) and we knew that as of midnight December 31, 1999, our existing system would no longer function properly.

This was a massive and critical conversion—think of it as changing out both engines of a 747, at the same time, while flying over the Atlantic Ocean.

And at this point, the conversion planning wasn't going well and we faced the risk that we could not complete the conversion on time.

So that's the challenge I faced as I stepped into this new role. And let me describe that first day on my new job so you get a sense of how lost, inadequate, and ill-equipped I felt stepping in to this new position.

The day of my official start date, I arrived at the office that had been assigned to me on the top floor of the building—a big, glamorous corner office. I'm a high-energy, action-oriented leader by nature, and understanding the hard work ahead of me I was eager to get started—to be introduced to my team, to review documents, to study operations reports, to go over financial reports, to meet my colleagues—all of the things you would typically do to get up to speed in a new role.

So imagine how lost I felt when I arrived at a mostly empty office, with nothing but a desk and a phone. No computer (and I didn't have a clue who to call to get one), no files, no reports or documents or org charts. And no one to ask for help—no assistant. Yet it was important I get to work immediately.

So I learned another lesson that I later called upon many times in my career—take it upon yourself to prepare *way* ahead of your first day on the job. Reach out, ask questions, meet key members of your team, get copies of reports and presentations, study org charts. There are so many ways you can do your homework so you can step into your new role with confidence, ready to hit the ground running. Lesson learned!

Once I was settled in, I dug in to the task of helping my team manage the system conversion. Imagine about 40 people all sitting around a big conference table in a room with white-board walls, and me, their brand new leader from outside the business, at the head of the table.

We met every day, a room full of "experts" trying to determine how to convert the data to work in the new system architecture. And we were stumped.

The problem was this team knew our current system inside out, and they hadn't been a part of the decision to purchase this new system. They were so constrained by, and loyal to, how our old system worked they could not open their minds to understand or even accept the functionality the new one offered, and therefore were unable to develop an effective data conversion plan.

So we huddled around that conference table day and night, making no progress. Every time I asked, "Why won't this new architecture work?" I'd get the same answer: "Because we don't do it that way."

They were back on their heels, arms crossed, defending the system they had built and managed all those years.

And every day the risk of failure was increasing as the Y2K deadline got closer and closer.

I kept trying desperately to learn enough about the system to be able to solve the problem myself—the way I was accustomed to working at the printing company—as the subject matter expert. But every night I went home exhausted, thinking, "How can I possibly give them the right answers or tell them how to solve this? They have all been doing this work for over 20 years. I'm not knowledgeable enough to solve this problem for them."

I even worried that my asking questions to enable me to learn about our system architecture would slow them down and derail them. Every night I went home feeling like a failure as a leader.

Until the night I went home and sat down to think about it, and I realized I had lost sight of the value that I, as a leader, brought to the team.

I wasn't asked to take on this role because I was an expert in systems architecture. I was asked to take on this role because I had a reputation as a strong leader who asked the right questions and learned quickly, who brought teams together to collaborate and innovate and challenge paradigms, and who was able to create a vision and inspire a team to do whatever it took to achieve that vision.

I resolved that starting the next day, I would stop trying to become the "expert" and I would start leveraging the leadership skills that got me to this position.

The next day I started with an exercise that eventually led to a breakthrough.

I realized I had to get the team to stop defending the way our current system worked, and I wasn't going to just magically convince them to embrace the new one.

So I started with a clean sheet of paper, a whiteboard, and I challenged the team like this. "If you, this team, was charged with creating a new system from scratch, what would it look like and how would it function?" A simple question that allowed them to set aside for a moment their comfort with the old system and their objections to the new system and simply create and brainstorm.

We spent a few days on this exercise, and I could see that it had lowered the tension in the room and even unleashed a little excitement and creativity.

Once we had the "ideal" system defined, I challenged them with another question—What are the critical differences between the new system and their "ideal" system? It was a pretty transparent question, they knew exactly where I was going, but as we dug in they couldn't deny that the new system was much, much closer to their ideal system than our old one was.

As we worked through each of the gaps between their "ideal" system and the new one, I asked questions like What are the ramifications of using this functionality as designed?" "What are the potential points of failure, the components that are truly incompatible with our business processes?" "How could we modify it to fit our needs?

"If we *had* to use it this way to meet the deadline, how would we make it work?"

It didn't happen overnight, but asking those simple questions led the team to set aside their biases and think creatively about how to tackle the conversion. I watched with pride as this incredible team of experts gradually took ownership of the new system and pulled out all the stops to develop a conversion plan that would work.

It took months of intense work, hundreds of people laboring day and night to convert the data and in some cases key it manually into the new system. People worked huge amounts of overtime, and worked through weekends to stay on schedule. We fueled their energy with tables full of pizzas and donuts and all kinds of snacks. We brought in a masseuse to give people neck and shoulder massages when they had spent too many hours in a row huddled over their keyboards. It was a team effort and every single person pitched in and did everything in their power to get the work done.

We managed to complete it on time, something we had at one time thought next to impossible. And I can tell you our big team had one heck of a celebration when January 1, 2000, arrived and the conversion was complete.

I learned another very valuable lesson in how I helped lead this team through the process of developing and executing the system conversion—

The more you advance through the ranks, the less likely you are to have all the answers. But you have to ask the right questions and be smart enough to recognize the right answer when you see it.

I didn't know enough to solve the problem for them, I had to rely on their expertise.

But asking the right questions was a critical part of getting to the right answer.

Over the years I've seen this play out time and time again with great leaders who have the confidence and the wisdom to ask questions.

There is tremendous value in a new set of eyes, a fresh perspective, and simple but insightful questions.

Work/Life Integration Is Personal

One of the questions I am most often asked when speaking to groups, particularly groups of women, is how I manage work/life balance.

The first thing I tell people is that we need to stop using the term "work/life balance," because it isn't like putting work on one end of a seesaw and life on the other end and then sitting very still so that it stays in balance. Not possible.

It's about integrating work into your life, and integrating life into your work, and the seesaw will not at times be evenly balanced in the middle, but in the course of a lifetime each side will dip and rise as you make trade-offs about your priorities and needs at various stages along the way.

I have a great deal of passion around this one. My family is the most important thing in my life. I'm a cancer survivor, so maintaining a healthy lifestyle is incredibly important to me.

I'm deeply spiritual, and believe that having the time to meditate, pray, or just be quiet and reflect on life is critical to living a fulfilling and purposeful life as well as maintaining health and well-being.

The term "work/life balance" is a throw-back to the days when work could be completed between the hours of nine to five, and then people went home to spend the evening in leisure activities with their families. There were no cell phones or connected devices—workers didn't have access to information about work once they left the office so they could *leave* work at the office and not pick it up again until the next day. There was no way to reach colleagues outside of the office except by calling their home phone, and that was typically reserved for real emergencies. So the hours outside of work—evenings and weekends—were truly hours that could be completely dedicated to families and leisurely pursuits. And work and life *were* fairly balanced.

Today, life is hectic and technology has resulted in an always-on, always-connected world. Lines between work and life blur. We don't just work when we're at the office, we work throughout the day, evening, and on weekends. Work is no longer contained to a specific time, and we struggle to find a way to fit "life" into the equation.

Today, the challenge is to achieve work/life *integration,* to make it all work together.

Integrating your work and your life is a process that starts with being grounded in your core values, setting goals, and prioritizing. And then it's a life-long process of making decisions and trade-offs with your priorities as your guiding star. Because you really can't do it all, all at the same time. You have to make choices.

And everyone's goals, priorities, and trade-offs are different.

Work/life integration isn't easy, and it takes deliberate focus, planning, and decision-making. But you can find the right way to make it work for you.

Over the years I've heard hundreds of women speak on the subject of integrating work and life. And I've heard hundreds of versions of how they have made it work.

There is no one way or right way to achieve it. Only you can decide what choices and trade-offs are right for you at any given point in your life. But hearing stories of how other women have managed work and life is helpful because there are some fundamental elements of effective work/life integration that are common across a majority of those stories.

The most common is the willingness to ask for help or hire help. This one seems so obvious, but I can tell you that in my experience, so many women are reluctant to do this, and the ones who do often don't really let go and let others help.

I was speaking to a young woman in my company a few years ago; we were having a discussion about her career. I'll call her Jessie here.

Jessie had just been promoted into a new role. It was a huge role for her, a critical set of finance responsibilities for the corporation, and she was leading a larger team than she had ever led before. She came to talk with me to ask my advice on getting up to speed in this new position and managing the hefty responsibilities of her new role. She wanted to make sure she was on track and doing all the right things to ensure success.

She was, not surprisingly, already working a lot of hours, far more hours than she was working in the job she had before. And she was worried about her ability to manage everything on her plate in this new role and still dedicate the time to her family that was so important to her.

Jessie has a wonderful husband with a successful career, and three terrific young children. Her husband's parents were retired and lived in the same city as Jessie and her family, but her parents lived several hours away in another state.

Jessie had no help at home. She and her husband were juggling the duties of getting their three children to and from school and all of their many activities, and generally doing all of the work to keep the household running.

I pointed out to Jessie that she would likely continue to have to work more hours in this new role. In addition, she was new to her organization and her boss, brand new to the work, and she needed to dedicate a little extra time early on to get up to speed so that she could establish her reputation and quickly deliver results. We talked about the fact that this was an important milestone in her career—it was the role she had hoped for and worked toward. If she delivered as expected in this role it would be a stepping stone to even bigger roles with broader responsibility.

I told her that this was the right time for her to sit down with her family and talk through their long-term goals and their priorities, and discuss some of the trade-offs that needed to be made if Jessie continued to advance to positions of greater responsibility. If her career was a priority for her and her family, now was the time to think about how she was going to manage everything going forward—all of her work responsibilities as well as all of her home and family life that was such an important priority for her.

I suggested that it was time to consider getting help at home, at the very least hiring someone to clean her house and eliminate that burden from her to-do list. I also proposed that she ask her in-laws, who lived close by and were retired, to help with her children one day/evening a week. It would allow her to work late without worrying about the kids and it would give the kids special time with their grandparents. And we talked about the fact that as her career continued to progress, an option might be to invest in a great nanny to provide after-school care for her children and dinners for her and her family.

She told me that she would feel guilty if she asked for help from her in-laws or hired a nanny, like she was delegating her duties as a mom. She felt she would be admitting that she couldn't handle the responsibilities of being a good parent while pursuing a career. She was adamant that she would find a way do it all.

Flash forward to a meeting I had with her almost a year later. She was running herself ragged, she was stressed, and she told me she didn't feel she was operating at 100% either at home *or* at work. She was getting her job done, but not to the best of her abilities. Her house was always a mess and she felt like she was spending less time with her family than ever. She always felt like she was behind, like she was scrambling to keep up, and she didn't feel like she was doing anything as well as she should.

I told her that by not getting the help she needed to manage everything on her plate, she had made *unintentional* or accidental trade-offs and sacrifices. Although her family was her highest priority, it seemed she had unintentionally sacrificed quality time with them more than anything else.

Work/life integration is about making *intentional* tradeoffs so that you remain in control of the choices you're making and the consequences of those trade-offs.

Jessie and I sat down and first made a list of the top five priorities in her life, in order, starting with her number one priority. For Jessie, that list was family, faith, health, career, and community. We then looked at a typical week on her calendar and highlighted the things that were in line with those five priorities to see if where she was actually spending her time was aligned with what she considered the most important things in her life.

I've often said that you can identify what you're *really* prioritizing by taking a look at an average week on your calendar.

Needless to say, this exercise was enlightening to Jessie. It showed her that only a minimal part of her time during the week was aligned with her priorities. Much of her work day was being consumed by meetings, not all of them essential, and not really contributing to her career development. Many of her nights were filled with the critical work that she couldn't get done during the day. Her evenings and weekends were packed with driving kids to activities, running errands, doing laundry, and keeping the house in order. Way too little of her weekly calendar included true quality time with her family.

This is a great exercise I suggest everyone do at least twice a year, and there are many online tools available to help, such as The Wheel of Life, or Steven Covey's Time Management Matrix. Search for "tools for setting priorities" and you'll find a wealth of information at your fingertips.

Once we completed the exercise, it was pretty clear to Jessie that many of the things that were lowest on her priority list could be delegated, outsourced, or managed in some creative ways that would free up her time for the highest priority items on her list.

For example, taking the kids to and from their numerous activities was not at the top of the list of quality time with the kids. It was hectic, rushed, the kids were distracted; it didn't allow for real quality conversation or time together. Jessie realized that working with other parents to develop carpool schedules would give her and her husband time to work late some evenings if they needed to, or time to occasionally have dinner together without the kids.

Jessie's workdays were filled with meetings that were scheduled by others and consumed a large portion of each day. Her presence wasn't critical in a lot of those meetings, so delegating some of the more routine ones to one or two of her top performers would give them terrific growth opportunities and free up some of her time to devote to more important work.

And housework and grocery shopping were at the very bottom of Jessie's list, so it was time to look for a solution there.

Jessie decided to hire a housekeeper who was also willing to do the grocery shopping once a week, which took a tremendous burden off of her shoulders. And she and her husband decided that it was time to look for a nanny who could ensure that the kids were cared for after school until she or her husband got home in the evening.

One tradeoff that they weren't willing to make was letting someone else cook dinner—she and her husband really loved cooking, and they always involved the kids, so it was a family activity they prioritized toward the top of their list. They developed a weekly schedule of which parent would get home each night in time to start dinner preparations with the kids. It required some juggling of work schedules for each of them on the nights when it was their turn, but it was worth it to them and turned out to be fun for the whole family to see what the assigned parent would put together for the family to whip up together each night.

These were a lot of major changes and a lot to take on for someone who was already overwhelmed, but Jessie and her husband realized these steps would greatly simplify their lives in the long run and they worked together to get them done. They all didn't happen overnight, but the most important thing is they did happen.

Jessie and her family made conscious decisions together about their priorities and the tradeoffs that were important to them so they could dedicate their time to the activities they valued most.

It all sounds so logical, but these are things I've seen women struggle with time and again—they feel they need to do it all, and when they try to do everything they find they are doing nothing really well.

You need to sit down and go through the exercise of listing all the activities you do on a daily or weekly basis. When you see the list, you'll realize why you're feeling overwhelmed. The world is much more complicated than it used to be, and we all have more activities, responsibilities, and options than we could ever possibly do in a day or a week. You need to prioritize to ensure you have time for the most important things in your life, and then you need to be creative about how you get help for the things at the bottom of your list.

One of the tradeoffs that some women seem reluctant to make is to decide that the husband, father, or partner should leave the workforce to be a stay-at-home parent. I've worked with many women whose husbands have chosen to be the primary care-giver and the arrangement has worked beautifully for their family. Some of my colleagues acknowledge that their husband is a better cook and loves it, he is more patient with the children, he loves spending days and evenings getting the kids to school and activities. It isn't the right solution for everyone, but it certainly is an option worth discussing. If you are one of the lucky women whose partner or husband is willing to make this choice, then rejoice and be proud—there are many women who would love to be in your shoes.

Don't be afraid to discuss options and ask for help.

And then be willing to accept the help that is offered.

I am guilty of not taking this advice myself. As a single mom early in my career, with my family and support system way across town, I often had the need to have someone help me by picking up my son after work and making sure he had a healthy meal while I was working late or taking my turn at covering part of the second shift. I had several friends, as well as the owner of the daycare center, who were always willing to help.

But even though others willingly, and gladly, offered to help, I made work for myself by feeling guilty, and not fully accepting the help they were offering.

One of my neighbors repeatedly offered to take my son home with her and get him dinner when I had to work late. When I had to take her up on it, I would stay up late the night before making a meal that I could send with my son the next day so that she didn't have to cook dinner for him. Not only did I spend the prior evening making a meal for my son, I made a meal for both of them.

Why? To relieve my guilt about asking for her help. To ensure that I wasn't placing an undue burden on her. To make sure I didn't feel like a bad mom.

She was more than willing to help me out, she lived alone and loved having my son's company, but instead of just accepting that help and letting a burden be lifted off of me, I created extra work and stress for myself.

I have a friend whom I've seen struggle with the same challenge of accepting help. Her husband works from home, and he is a terrific husband and father. He does his best to do his share of taking care of the household and the children. He is always understanding when my friend, Cara, has to travel or has an evening commitment. He truly doesn't feel it's extra work for him, and he enjoys his "special" time with the kids.

Whenever Cara is going to be gone for an evening or a few days, however, she spends days making lists and getting her husband prepared to manage without her. She does the grocery shopping and prepares meals in advance and lays out what meal is to be eaten each night. She lays out the kids clothes for every day that she will be gone, actually packing whole outfits into large plastic baggies to ensure that her husband doesn't have to search for matching tights or baseball socks. She calls other moms and lines up rides for the kids to and from their evening activities. She makes a tremendous amount of additional, unnecessary work and stress for herself, when her husband is perfectly capable and willing to handle it on his own.

And Cara takes it one step further when she returns home from a trip. Before her plane hits the ground she is already whipping herself up into a frenzy about all the work that she just knows awaits her at home. She hits the door and looks right past the fact that the kids are well fed and happy and homework is done, instead focusing on the dishes in the sink, the chocolate ice cream on the counter, and the clothes on the floor. She is immediately a whirlwind of activity, running around picking things up and getting the house back in order. Her husband always says to her—you go relax and spend time with the kids, I'll go take care of everything else that needs to be done. But she can't let go and accept the help.

Do you see yourself in Cara?

Think about these three tips as you work to integrate work and life:

- Get comfortable with asking for help, or hiring help
- Consider all options, including a spouse or partner who is the primary care-giver while you are the primary bread-winner
- When help is offered, accept it and let go of the guilt and perfectionism

When people ask me if I believe it's possible to have it all, I say that I believe you can have it all, just not necessarily all at the same time.

You need to start with the process of figuring out what is important. If you let work just sweep you along it's like stepping on a long moving sidewalk that starts moving faster and faster and there are no logical places to exit. If you do that, you are unintentionally sacrificing some of the most important things in your life because you haven't taken the step to intentionally prioritize and think through the trade-offs you're willing to make.

I believe "having it all" needs to be redefined. My definition of having it all is this:

At all times in my life, keeping my values, goals, and priorities in sight to ensure that I'm dedicating time to the most important things in my life. At different points in my life I will make conscious choices and trade-offs, but at the end of my life I will be able to look back and say, "I don't regret what I did or didn't do. I made trade-offs along the way but I'm content with the trade-offs I made. I didn't sacrifice the most important things in my life. I was passionate about and achieved my definition of success. I made the best use of my unique God-given gifts and I made a difference in the lives of others."

There will be times in your life when your family needs and activities just come first. Period. When the most important thing in the world to you is being there for baseball games or dance recitals, or for homework every night. During those times, you might have to make some trade-offs at work. You might need to ask for a smaller set of responsibilities, or turn down a promotion or a new project. You might even have to consider a downgrade. That's ok, because you are doing what is right for you, taking care of your priorities, and consciously making the trade-offs that work for you.

At other points in your life you might make a different set of trade-offs. What if you are offered a significant promotion, the one you've been hoping for, but you know it is going to require some longer hours as you get up to speed? What if you're offered the opportunity to work on a special project that requires travel but that will give you high visibility and the experience you need to go for that next promotion?

You have decisions to make, and you need to make them intentionally and with the full involvement and support of your family and significant others.

This is where you sit down at home and discuss the options and implications. If you and your family and significant others decide that this is an opportunity you can't pass up, that it's the opportunity you've been waiting for and it puts you on the career path you all agree is worth some short-term trade-offs, then you need to have an honest conversation about what those trade-offs are. You are all in this together.

This might be when you decide it's time to hire help, or time to take your parents up on their offer to help. It's when you explain to the kids that Mommy has an exciting new job and will be working longer hours for a while but will make sure she is home on the weekends and that will be our family time together. You get the picture. Make sure everyone has the right expectations going in, eyes wide open, and you'll find the trade-offs easier to manage.

One bit of advice I have given over the years to anyone who is facing a big new opportunity that will require long hours and a lot of stress—have an ending in sight.

I personally think it's not fair to sign up for an assignment, ask your family to support you while you devote more time to work, and not be able to tell them how long they'll have to endure it. You and your family can manage through anything for a period of time, but they have to know there is a light at the end of the tunnel, that relief is coming. *You* have to know there is a light at the end of the tunnel.

No job or new assignment is worth burning yourself out, losing your health, or losing your family.

Stay grounded in your goals, values, and life priorities, and find the work/life integration that works for you. Be relentless about keeping your activity aligned with your priorities. And never feel guilty about dedicating time to the highest priorities in your life.

Humility - Never Make the Mistake of Thinking It Is All About You.

In his book, *The One Minute Manager*, Ken Blanchard states, "People with humility do not think less of themselves; they just think about themselves less."

When we think about strong leaders, we typically think of leaders with strength, charisma, decisiveness, and high self-confidence, who are expert problem-solvers. We don't automatically think of humility in that list of traits.

But without humility, that list of traits can easily describe a top-down, autocratic style of leadership that causes teams to disengage and wait to be told what to do.

Research has shown that managers who exhibit traits of humility—such as seeking feedback and focusing on the needs of others—drive higher employee engagement and job performance. That's important to note—it's not just employee engagement that's at stake, it's performance and results.

In my own experience, I've seen this to be true time and time again.

Humility makes us more human. Without humility, we will walk around believing we're infallible, that we have all the answers, that we're the smartest person in the room. That tends to create distance between us and others, between us and our team.

Being a humble leader doesn't mean lacking confidence or being wishy-washy or working too hard to get to consensus rather than exhibiting strong leadership.

Being humble means being *secure and confident* enough to admit you don't have all the answers, being open to others' opinions, and truly listening to and caring about others' input and needs. Humble leaders realize that no one is ever a perfectly finished work of art; they are self-aware and practice self-reflection and ongoing development and course-correction.

Humble leaders are willing to teach, enable, and equip their people, communicate a vision and direction, and then get out of their way and let them do their jobs. They are willing to let people learn from their mistakes, and grow their own wings.

One of the best bosses I ever had, and one of the most highly respected leaders in our business at the time, was also a very humble leader.

Mike was a seasoned professional who had worked for the company for over 20 years. He had worked his way up through the organization and had experience in almost every business unit, with an outstanding track record of delivering results. He was a senior executive running an organization of more than 50,000 people, and he had full P&L responsibility.

Mike was one of the smartest people I had ever worked for. He knew so much about every part of the business, and he never met a fact or a data point that he didn't file away for instant access at any time.

He was adept at understanding and running operations, and he was the rare combination of tactical and strategic—he was willing to get down in the details and work through issues and challenges, and he was also an incredible visionary. He wasn't just looking out at the horizon, he had the ability to see *past* the horizon and lay out a strategic framework and plan for us to get there before our competition.

It could have been intimidating working for a leader like Mike. But on the contrary, it was empowering. Because Mike didn't feel the need to constantly demonstrate how smart he was—he was more focused on driving results by leveraging all the talent on the team, helping people grow and learn, and sharing the credit.

While I was working for Mike, part of my responsibility was for strategic planning for our organization. He gave me the task of developing a strategic five-year plan for our organization.

I had a team of outstanding people working for me, and we were energized about our task of determining how our organization would evolve over the next five years—the capabilities that emerging technology would enable, the impact on headcount and cost and the customer experience, and the financial impact those changes would have. We set about the task of developing the plan with gusto.

Mike took a hands-off approach, giving us high level direction and then turning us loose to do our research and analysis—to do our job. I checked in with Mike frequently, bringing him up to speed on the status of various aspects of the plan. When we reached various decision points I sat down to talk through options and pros and cons with him. And when problems or obstacles arose I enlisted his help and input.

When the plan was completed I sat down to review it with Mike. Our work had taken us down a path we hadn't expected, and resulted in a set of outcomes and recommendations that neither I nor my team had anticipated when we started the project, so I expected Mike to be surprised at, or even want to debate, the final recommendations we were making. But when I finished reviewing it with him, giving him all the rationale and working to convince him that we needed to take the direction the team was recommending, he said, "This is pretty much where I thought you might end up."

I was surprised and a little put off by his response, and I asked him why he let us go do all that work, and explore an exhaustive list of options, if he had an idea of where he thought our analysis would take us all along.

And he said because if he had told us what he was thinking we would have taken his lead and we wouldn't have explored all of the options with an open mind, and he wanted all of the options studied and tested. If he had just given us the answer, we wouldn't have learned and grown through the process of doing all the analysis. And he said he trusted us to do the work and come to our own conclusion, even at the risk that our conclusion might be different from what he expected.

I call that a humble leader. He wasn't so full of ego that he thought he had all the answers. He didn't arrogantly believe his opinion was always right. He didn't feel the need to constantly show people that he was the smartest person in the room.

He was secure and self-confident enough to give high level direction and then get out of the way and let us do our job. He listened to my input, debated with me, sometime changing my direction and at times adjusting his expectations of the outcome. He was willing to give me and my team credit for the final product and the brilliance of the plan. He never stopped leading, he just didn't make it all about him, he made it all about us and the work we did.

I learned more working for Mike than perhaps any other leader I had worked for up to that point. Because he was willing to teach, empower, turn people loose, and let people fail as a way of learning. And he was willing to be open to an outcome that might be different from the one he was expecting.

Jim Collins, author of *Good to Great*, one of my favorite books on leadership, said, "The X-factor of great leadership is not personality. It's humility."

Networking Isn't a Dirty Word, It Is Critical to Getting Things Done and Getting Opportunities

One of the most distinct and profound lessons I've learned by looking back over my career journey and the opportunities I've had along the way, is the importance of having a network. I would not have had many of the opportunities that came my way if it hadn't been for my network. I would never have achieved my dream without the help and support of my network.

In my experience, men tend to be much better at developing the *right* network than women.

Women tend to believe that work should be a meritocracy--if you work hard, keep your head down and do a great job of leading teams and delivering results you'll be noticed, rewarded, and selected for new opportunities. They often view networking as a distasteful task, as "working the system," as being disingenuous. They struggle with how to build a network in a way that feels comfortable to them. But I passionately believe that networking, done right, is not distasteful or disingenuous, and is absolutely critical to getting things done and opening the doors of opportunity.

When I was working at the publishing division of BellSouth, I was far removed from the core operations of the telephone company business. We had very little reason to interact with our telco peers, and our offices were across town from the headquarters campus so there was no opportunity for even casual interaction.

I was running all the call center operations for the publishing company at the time, and there was no one else who really knew call center operations, no one at my division that I could benchmark with or learn from. I was always interested in learning and discovering ways to improve my operations, so I looked across to the telephone company to see who I might be able to connect and collaborate with.

I asked a number of people who the best call center operator was in the business, and one name emerged as an outstanding leader of call centers. So I reached out to Bob, told him who I was, and asked if he would be willing to spend a little time with me sharing best practices and ideas about call center management. We set up a time to meet for lunch.

I learned a great deal during that lunch, and I hope Bob might have gotten a few nuggets from me as well because he initiated the next meeting, and after that we met about once a quarter to catch up, share best practices, and generally philosophize about call center management.

Bob knew more about call center operations than anyone I knew. He had a deep understanding of the critical metrics that drove operational performance and cost. He understood customer needs and was a tireless advocate for the customer. And he cared deeply about people.

Bob drove results like nobody's business—sales, customer satisfaction, cost reduction—but he was also a leader that people really wanted to work for because he was an honest, transparent, and humble leader who genuinely cared about doing the right thing for the customer, the business, and the people. And he consistently led winning teams. I treasured my lunches with Bob and I learned so much from just listening to his stories about challenges he faced as a call center leader and the ways he addressed and overcame them.

Many years later, when I was in a very different role in a different part of the business and he and I had to some degree lost touch, I got a call from Bob. He had just been promoted, and he said, "I have a job open, running call centers in the core part of the business. It's a big job and I have a long line of people who have put their names in the hat for the position. But from all of those lunches we had, I know how you run call centers and I know how you treat people, and there's no one I'd rather see in this job than you."

Of course I said yes. I was honored and thrilled to be offered that opportunity, and that job turned out to be one of the favorite roles of my career.

It's a great example of a job opportunity that came to me because of a contact in my network, one that I had established years ago.

One other example from earlier in my career is an even more profound illustration of the value of a network.

I was still with the publishing company at this time, VP of Operations, still far removed from the core operations of the business. I got a call one day from the SVP of Network Operations—he led the entire network operation for the company. I knew who Richard was, but I had never met him. He said he had a VP job in network operations that he wanted to talk with me about, and we set up a meeting for the next day in his office.

When I hung up the phone I thought to myself, That's really nice, I'm probably on some list and someone asked him to do a courtesy interview with me. Because I had never even been *close* to network operations in my whole career, I thought there was probably no way he was really considering me for the job.

I went to meet with Richard the next day and we were about 20 minutes into our conversation when he said, "Let me just make sure you're clear about why you're here."

I thought, Here it comes, this is where he says this was a nice chance to get to know you but you're not really qualified for the job.

But to my surprise, he said, "This isn't about me interviewing you for this job. This job is yours if you want it. This is about you deciding if you want to take it."

I was stunned. I said, "Why me?"

He told me that what he needed in this role was someone with three distinct leadership qualities:

- The ability to roll up your sleeves and get in the trenches and learn quickly, see the big picture, and significantly improve the efficiency and effectiveness of any team or organization

- The ability to create a vision that a large team of employees and contractors can rally around and get behind, and the willingness to bust through walls to make things happen
- The ability to collaborate across a very diverse set of functions and leaders and a challenging set of personalities, bringing them together to align around a common set of goals and an agreed-upon path forward

He said that as he interviewed people and talked to others about what he was looking for, he was surprised at how many people said, "That's Debbie Storey. You need to talk to her."

That was the moment I realized I had built a powerful network over time, and that network was working for me even when I wasn't in the room.

I also realized that I had built a reputation, or a personal brand—a promise of the skills and capabilities I would bring to every role I stepped in to. And my network of mentors and sponsors had so clearly conveyed my brand to Richard that he was convinced my skills and capabilities were the right fit for the role he was seeking to fill.

I took the job working for Richard in the network organization. That job turned out to be one of the most challenging roles in my career, but it also resulted in tremendous growth because it took me so far out of my comfort zone. Richard was an outstanding leader—tough but fair, demanding but supportive—he pushed me hard and demanded a lot, but I always knew he had my back. I learned so much from him, and after I moved on to another role he remained one of my trusted mentors. He has since retired, and I received a text from him recently that said, "Never forget you're a champion." Richard will always be one of my treasured champions and role models.

My relationships with Richard and Bob are examples of the network of diverse leaders I had developed naturally and organically over the years. I had built relationships in a way that was comfortable to me, without any kind of distasteful "networking."

I had simply reached out to meet with leaders to learn about different parts of the business. I had collaborated with peers when I saw "white space" between our groups and wanted to work together to fix a gap. I had connected with others by volunteering for projects and committees that allowed people all over the business to get to know me and see my work.

I had done that hundreds of times, and these are just two examples of the many times that network resulted in an opportunity being directed my way. A powerful illustration of why you want to focus on building your network.

One of the mistakes I think people make when it comes to networking is believing that it's all about seeking out people at higher levels than you. There is no question that you need to have a few well-placed people in your network, and at least one sponsor who is in a position of influence. But in my career, almost every single opportunity that has come to me has been because of a relationship I established with a peer. Over time those peers moved into positions of influence and were willing to direct opportunities my way.

You should consider the possibility that the person sitting in the cube next to you today may one day be the head of a business unit who needs someone just like you for a big role. I've seen it happen. Start building your network now.

I said in the beginning of this section that in my experience, men do a better job of building effective networks than women. Let me describe what that difference is, based on the men and women I've worked with over the years.

Men tend to naturally think in terms of a network, or a "team." They want to be on a good team, a winning team, and they know that in sports, when you "play up" you improve your own skills and abilities. So they naturally seek out others to be on their team who are more skilled, more connected, more powerful. And they have no qualms about asking others for help, for favors. They actually expect to be brought along by their "team members" in their network. That's just what a network is to them.

Women have a tendency to seek relationships at work that provide them with support. They seek out others who are in similar situations, positions and levels so they can comfortably share challenges and accomplishments, can commiserate and celebrate together. They tend to be less willing to call on others to do favors for them, and when they do need help from someone to get a new opportunity or a promotion, they typically don't have people in their networks who are in powerful enough positions to help.

Many studies have shown that women typically have more mentors than men, but men's mentors tend to be in more senior levels and more likely to be able to provide sponsorship. There's an important distinction between a mentor and a sponsor. A mentor coaches you and gives advice, helps you learn and grow and deal with specific challenges you bring to them. A sponsor is typically someone who is a few levels higher than you and well-placed, someone who can give you a broader perspective on the business, make connections for you, and open doors for you.

A mentor talks to you, a sponsor talks about you.

In order for women to continue to advance, we *have* to learn to be good at building powerful and strategic networks and at seeking out sponsors, not just acquiring networks of people who look just like us. And then we have to get over our reluctance to ask people in our network for help and support in seeking new opportunities.

Lots of people have asked me how you go about building a network—they say they don't even know where to begin. I think it doesn't have to be that difficult, but it does take a little thought, planning, and follow-through.

Following are some of the ways you can make new connections and build your network without it feeling uncomfortable or disingenuous:

- My first piece of advice here, and perhaps the most important, is that as you reach out to make new connections, don't ask for an hour of someone's time. Busy leaders don't have open hours on their schedule. Ask for 15 minutes of their time. Who can say no to a request to spend 15 minutes helping you learn about the business? And people don't typically schedule their calendar in 15-minute increments, so chances are you'll have up to 30 minutes if the conversation goes well.
- Reach out to other leaders doing similar work to yours—peers, those at higher levels of management, and even those at a lower level—and invite them to get together and share best practices, to see what you can learn from each other. Every one of these connections has the potential to connect you to others who might become a valuable part of your network.
- Join employee resource groups or clubs at work. Many of those are sponsored by senior leaders. Volunteer to take on some meaningful work that will allow you to engage with those senior leaders. Lead projects or committees so people have the opportunity to see your leadership in action. That's a terrific way to build your reputation, your personal brand.
- Ask people to make introductions for you. Yes, you have to be willing to ask for help. One of the mentors in your network certainly has a connection to a senior leader,

and would be more than happy to make an introduction for you.

- Reach out to a leader and ask for an informational meeting. Ask them to spend 15 minutes with you to help you learn about their part of the business. And then prepare thoroughly to ensure that your meeting goes well.

I have a few key tips on this one that are critical to the success of these meetings. When a senior leader agrees to meet with you, you *owe* them the courtesy of making the meeting easy for them. Do your homework and come prepared with a *brief* overview of what you do and what you're passionate about, where you'd like to go in your career, and then have a set of prepared questions that you want to ask the leader.

Ensure the first few questions you ask are about their work or their career or their passion—every leader loves the opportunity to talk about those things. The time will fly by and the meeting will feel effortless to the leader. And you've just planted the seeds of a relationship that has the potential to grow into a mentoring relationship.

I've had people I've never met before ask for time on my calendar and then arrive in my office, sit down, and say, "I just wanted to get some advice from you on how to get promoted." Then the entire 30-minute conversation is mine to manage, and it's work for me. And I'm not likely to agree to meet with the person again. If you come prepared and make it effortless for the leader, you will leave a good impression, they will be willing to connect you with others, and you will likely have an opportunity for another meeting with them in the future.

One way you might think about building your network is to frame it in terms of a personal board of directors. If you were a CEO, building your board, you would be looking for 10 or 12 directors who each bring a unique set of experiences, characteristics, and skills to your team of advisors. You're the CEO of You, so you need your own board of trusted advisors.

You need people on your board who bring a broad spectrum of experience, who are from various parts of the business and from different backgrounds, age groups, and ethnic groups. You need mentors and sponsors who stretch you in new ways, who help you think differently, who help you grow and learn about other parts of the business, who bring perspectives that are different from yours. Having someone on your board from outside your business also brings a unique outlook to your board. Diversifying your network allows you to tap into wisdom you normally would not have access to, and develop a support infrastructure to help you succeed and advance.

Limiting your network to one or two people in high level positions can leave you without a sponsor if they leave or fall out of favor. If you only have people in your network who are just like you, you run the risk that they will tell you only what you want to hear rather than helping you get out of your comfort zone and try new things. Building a broad and diverse board of directors is the key to having a strong set of advisors throughout your career.

There are many other creative ways to build your network. One of my colleagues, Rachel, has developed a practice that is not only effective at expanding her network, but is fun for her and for those she connects with. Here is her technique.

A few years ago, she reached out to Mary—a woman in another part of the business at the same level as Rachel, whom she didn't know, and she invited Mary to lunch so they could get to know each other. Everyone eats lunch, so inviting someone to lunch is a great way to connect with a new contact.

At that lunch Rachel pitched her networking proposal to Mary, which would require the two of them to collaborate going forward.

Every month the two of them would meet for lunch, and each of them would invite another woman she didn't know well. Each month this lunch foursome would create two new connections for Rachel and Mary, but would also create *three* new connections for the new women invited to join that month. A beautiful way for women to help each other expand their network in a way that is actually fun and non-intimidating.

Make connections naturally and let them grow organically and it won't feel uncomfortable to you; you might even find it fun and you will certainly find it helps expand your knowledge of the business. But be strategic about those connections. Your goal is to build a network that will work for you, even when you're not in the room.

Default to YES!

A senior executive I know in another company is the CFO, and he often tells a story about one of his female colleagues as a way of explaining the value of defaulting to Yes.

This CFO, Mitch, had a challenge arise that he needed to address quickly. One of his divisions, in another state, was experiencing significant issues and he needed a seasoned leader to go be on-site in another city for for a few months to help straighten them out. He knew exactly who was the right person with the right skills and background for the job.

He went to Marcy's office to talk to her about it. He explained the problem, and said he needed someone with the right combination of financial and business operations experience to go be on-sight to help get this division back on course. He explained that it would be a tough and challenging assignment, high risk, but a lot of visibility and high reward if this leader was successful.

He said I want you to do it.

Mitch knew that Marcy had young children at home and her husband traveled for work. He knew she had no family close by who could easily pitch in and help. But he was a huge champion of Marcy's, he knew just how capable and talented she was, and he knew she wanted to be in the CFO role one day. He not only felt strongly that she was the right person to pull this division out of the ditch, but he knew it would catapult her into the career path she wanted.

Marcy hesitated for maybe a minute and then said YES, I'll do it.

As Mitch tells the story, he acknowledges that Marcy had no idea how she would make it work, and she went home that night with a lot of logistics to figure out.

Marcy came back two days later and said, "I've talked it over with my family and I know I can do this. I've been reviewing the budgets and income statements and I can already see opportunities to begin to right the ship. I can be on sight three days a week, my best friend will loan me her nanny for those days for the next three months, and longer if I need it. On Mondays and some Fridays I will work from here, and I know I can get the job done."

Mitch agreed, Marcy turned the division around in a little more than three months, and two years later she was the CFO of her own business unit.

Mitch's point in telling that story is that most of us, when faced with a challenge that feels too big, or a set of circumstances we don't know how we'll manage, immediately say no. He was challenging us to default to yes, and then figure out how to make it work even if it involves compromise.

Men have an advantage when the high risk, high profile opportunities come along. They don't stop to say "Am I qualified?" They don't stop to say "How will I balance everything?" They say yes, and then go figure out how to make it happen.

When more women are willing to say YES! to the high profile, high powered assignments and then figure out how to make it happen, more women will build the credentials and the reputation that will position them for roles at the top.

But this doesn't just apply to really big assignments and opportunities, it applies to other decisions we make. Lateral moves, new assignments, projects, promotions, even life decisions—some of us have a tendency to pause and think of all the reasons we can't do it.

One of the reasons women sometimes put opportunities and decisions on hold is because of the events that might happen in the future—the "what if's."

Kelly is one of the women I've mentored over the years. She is in her late 20s and has a great job with the company. She is smart, engaging, quick, and has excelled in every role she has been in. She asked to meet with me because she was at a crossroads and wanted to talk about some decisions she was wrestling through.

Kelly has a bachelor's degree and she was considering going back to school to get her master's degree. I am a huge fan of education and I believe a master's degree is a great decision for anyone who has been in the workforce three to five years and wants to continue to advance.

When I gave Kelly that feedback she said, "I just don't know if now is the right time. I think my boyfriend might propose in the next year, I'm not sure I want to be planning a wedding and going to school at the same time. And then if we decide to have children, it would be hard for me to finish school. Maybe it would be better to wait until after I have children and go back to school then." She wasn't even engaged yet and she was making a critical decision based on the "what if's."

She was also wrestling with financial decisions—she wanted to buy a house and stop paying rent, but "What if my boyfriend proposes and we want to buy a house together?"

I tried my best to encourage Kelly to decide what she wanted to do and move forward with it, not wait on an action that might happen at some undetermined time. I told her there is really no perfect time to go back to school, you just have to jump in and do it. And I told her I thought it would only get tougher if she was married and had children.

When I realized I wasn't succeeding in giving her the courage to move forward, I suggested that she sit down and talk through it with her boyfriend so they could make decisions about their future together. She was uncomfortable with that as well; she didn't want to spoil the surprise if he was thinking about proposing sometime soon. So I left that conversation knowing that Kelly was putting her life on hold waiting for something that might or might not happen.

I saw Kelly a year later, and was disappointed to learn that she was still not engaged, still hadn't bought a house, and was still wrestling with the decision of whether to get her master's. She could have been almost half through with it by then, but she was paralyzed by the "what if's" that still hadn't happened yet.

Maybe this is an extreme example, but I've seen women time and again lean back and be reluctant to make life decisions or pursue new work opportunities because of the "what if's" they are focused on. It's one of the things that keeps women from advancing early in their career.

If you have the right skills and the right network, if you have the right sponsors and support group, if you have the right help in place to allow you to manage work and life well—

Default to YES! And then gather your resources and figure out how to make it happen. Make the decisions to move forward with your career and life, and if your life changes—if you get married, get pregnant, have to move—trust me, you'll figure it out then. People always do.

Never Mistake Kindness for Weakness

Strong leadership and kindness are not mutually exclusive. In fact, kindness *amplifies* power, it doesn't diminish it. The most successful leaders treat their team members with kindness, care, and genuine concern. They realize that *kindness is motivating.*

Kindness isn't about being nice. It's about genuinely caring about people while you lead with strength, authenticity, and humility.

Kind leaders drive impressive results, in the *right* way. They set high expectations for their team, they hold people accountable, and then they roll up their sleeves and get in the trenches with them. They listen to the input of their people and pay attention to the unique challenges facing them. They don't ignore obstacles or conflicts, they face them head on and deal with them.

Kind leaders are willing to take the blame when things go wrong and give their team the credit when things go right.

But kind leaders also firmly manage performance; they understand that giving feedback, coaching and mentoring are acts of kindness. Helping people to grow, develop, and fix fatal flaws is a responsibility of all leaders, but can be done in a way that is respectful and constructive. Everyone respects a boss who cares enough to help you get better.

I had a recent conversation with two of my former employees who made me realize just how powerful kindness and respect can be. Paula and Sam worked for me at the same time many years ago; they were part of my support team. I was having dinner with them recently and they told a story about a time when I gave them feedback in a subtle but powerful way.

They said they were in my office late one evening and we were reviewing an aspect of the business that wasn't going well, and I was frustrated that we hadn't realized it and reacted sooner. We spent a good hour going over every detail of what had gone wrong, and talking step by step about how we had gotten there. We talked about the warning signs we should have seen but missed, and we went over what we would do differently to avoid it happening again. We worked painstakingly through various scenarios of how we could get back on track. And we ultimately agreed on an action plan, to be implemented immediately, that would get us quickly back on course.

As Paula recounted the story, she said she and Sam walked back to their offices, quietly thinking through the intense conversation we had just had. They got all the way to their offices, and Paula paused, turned to Sam and said, "Did we just get chewed out?"

Sam stopped, cocked his head, looked at her for a moment and said, "I think we did!"

They looked at each other and said, "We just got chewed out!" They vowed never to have that happen again, and they stayed late that night talking through their plan to swiftly get us back on track.

If I had actually chewed them out, yelled at them and ranted about how could you let this happen and what are you going to do about it, they would have walked back to their offices feeling beat up and defeated. They agreed that they probably would have just left the office to go home and lick their wounds.

Instead, I treated them with respect. They were talented leaders, and I knew they already felt terrible about the position we had gotten ourselves into—I didn't need to beat them up any further than they were already beating themselves up. Instead, I focused our discussion on reviewing how we got here—so we could learn from this mistake—and then on solutions to recover quickly.

I was firm with them, making it clear that we had gone off track and my expectation was that we would fix it quickly and learn from this situation. They knew, without my demeaning them by ranting or berating them, that they had disappointed me, and in their words, they "never wanted to let that happen again."

The 13th century Persian poet, Rumi, wrote: "Raise your voice, not your words. It's the rain that grows flowers, not thunder..."

The best leaders understand that we rise by lifting others, not beating others down. People need that sense of gratification that comes from being respected and trusted, from being recognized for the unique contributions they bring to the workforce every day.

This is more true today than it has ever been. Life is hectic in this always-on, always-connected world. Lines between work and life blur. We need emotional gratification from all parts of our life, and that includes the many waking hours we are connected to, and engaged with, work activities.

Job fulfillment, how leaders make people feel about their jobs and their work, is more critical than ever before and even an essential part of life because work is such a *huge* part of our lives today. Managing it all is tough, and having a boss who cares about us, our well-being, our work-life integration, our growth, is an increasingly important thread in the complex fabric of our lives. It can make the difference between dreading getting up in the morning and going to work, and actually looking forward to the camaraderie, the collaboration and achievement of big things, and the recognition that follows.

A kind leader realizes that work is hard and hours can be long, and it is critical that we take the time to "make it personal" and have fun at work. She realizes that mistakes will happen, and people need to be held accountable, learn from them, and fix them, but that public execution for an honest mistake doesn't motivate or inspire anyone to rise and do better next time. It only motivates them to avoid ever being caught making a mistake again.

Many people fail to understand that basic leadership concept—that leadership style truly matters. It's not just how talented or educated the leader is or how much they know. It's ultimately how they treat people that matters. In the end, a leader's style is the difference between a team that punches the clock, and a team that will willingly and gladly follow the boss into battle and go the extra mile to achieve the vision.

Kind leaders consistently inspire people to fully commit themselves to the work in front of them, and the vision that has been laid out for them. These leaders create followers who are willing to walk through walls for their bosses, customers, co-workers, and the company.

Tyrannical, autocratic leaders—many of them highly intelligent, strategic, and successful leaders—drain the energy from the room and demotivate people to the point that they are willing to do only what is required to stay off the radar and keep their jobs.

Leaders who take a genuine interest in their people, who treat people with respect and care, affect others so deeply that they develop an intrinsic motivation to produce, excel, and achieve more than is expected.

Because the foundation of human motivation is more than metrics and scorecards and compensation, it is the reward of meaningful work - of being seen as an individual, recognized for your unique contributions, and emotionally connected to the work and the leadership.

I have been fortunate to work with many strong but kind bosses over the years. I have also worked in organizations led by an autocratic leader who ruled using "position power" and authority.

When I was running an operations team at one point in my career, a restructure resulted in our organization reporting to a new leader, whom I'll call Steve. Steve had held many different leadership positions within the company; he had tremendous breadth and depth of knowledge of the business and was probably one of the smartest people in the company. But Steve was an autocratic leader who ruled using position power. He had a reputation of not being collaborative and not having genuine concern for people; instead he treated them like instruments to be used to achieve his objectives.

When my organization started reporting in to him, he immediately began to make significant changes in the way we operated, slashing budgets and reducing our allotted headcount. He didn't get the team together, discuss what needed to change and why, and allow us to have some input into those changes. Instead, he gave orders, dictated the changes and kept enough distance from the troops that he didn't have to hear the angst or see the confusion and dysfunction that some of his decisions drove. Without context, people didn't understand what he was trying to accomplish with the changes. Without discussion, people were unable to give feedback, they felt like pawns in his chess game, waiting to be told where to move next. Without recognition for what they had accomplished in the past and what they were going through to carry out his directives, the team felt unappreciated and increasingly demoralized.

Steve came across as arrogant—he didn't seem to understand or even care about the dynamics that were playing out among his team as he rewarded those who followed without questioning, and publicly chastised those who pushed back or offered an opinion that differed from his. Energy was sapped as people commiserated about the negative culture that his leadership style was breeding; they lost the drive and motivation to be creative or innovative. Everyone dreaded meetings with him, knowing they would be tested and challenged at every turn.

Steve intimidated people into action, he beat people down as a way to assert authority and ensure people were driven to do only what he demanded. Eventually people began looking for a way out of his organization. For the first time in my career, I began to consider looking for a position outside the company.

"Sometimes our light goes out but is blown again into flame by an encounter with another human being. Each of us owes the deepest thanks to those who have rekindled this inner light."
Albert Schweitzer, French-German theologian.

Thankfully, Steve moved on to a new opportunity outside the company, and we began reporting to a different leader who was smart, knowledgeable, driven, and genuinely cared about people. Danny was a strong and successful leader who understood that kindness is motivating.

Danny got us all together—his entire leadership team—to talk about where we were as an organization, sort of a "state of the union" meeting. He listened as we talked with pride about our accomplishments, and he also listened as the team raised concerns about some of the decisions that had previously been made that were driving the wrong behaviors and results. He asked great questions, he drew out the opinions and input of his team around the table, and then he gave direction on how we were going to operate going forward, and the kind of culture we were going to create.

The team left that very first meeting with our new leader feeling energized and excited—we had someone at the helm who listened, treated us with genuine respect and concern, but who would clearly drive us to set high goals and hold us accountable for achieving results.

Danny rekindled the flame that our previous leader had almost extinguished.

Danny led in a way that motivated people—driving the business forward to achieve incredible things by inspiring his team, unleashing the capabilities of every member of the team, and creating an environment in which people felt that their contributions were valued and recognized. He constantly placed the needs of the business and the people above his own ambitions and need for recognition. He built people up to inspire and motivate them. He created a winning team, and we all loved being a part of it.

Danny's team would have walked through walls for him, and under his leadership we consistently delivered amazing results that exceeded all expectations.

I once had the honor of meeting Madeleine Albright, and although I've never seen this quoted anywhere else, in that meeting she captured the essence of humble leadership this way:

"Extraordinary leaders awaken in us the courage we forgot we had, and inflame us to take action. They are successful not so much for what *they* know and do, but for what they inspire *others* to do."

Humble leaders don't have to constantly *prove* what *they* know and can do, they are confident enough to lift others up and share the credit.

That's the kind of boss most people want to work for.

Be the kind of leader that people want to work for.

Chapter 7:

Driving Results – My 5 C's of Leadership

Up to now I've talked about the softer aspects of leadership, the qualities that make a good leader great. Now let's talk about how you put all these terrific leadership qualities in action to deliver results.

For many years, as I have helped new supervisors and managers make the transition from being an individual contributor to a leader who gets things done through others, I have used what I call my 5 C's of Leadership to help them understand how the most successful leaders lead teams to drive results.

My 5 C's of Leadership:

- CREATE a vision
- CONNECT people to the vision
- COACH people to success
- CHALLENGE the team to deliver even more
- CELEBRATE...give credit and recognition freely

Let me talk about each of the 5 C's and give examples of how effective leaders put them into action.

If you follow these 5 C's, you will be well on your way to being the kind of leader people want to follow—you will never have to look back to see if people are following, you will have to keep moving fast to ensure they don't get ahead of you!

1. CREATE a vision

People can't follow you if they don't know where you're trying to lead them. Without a vision, your team is like a ship that is traveling aimlessly through the water, making a lot of waves, but unable to see the lighthouse that will lead it safely to its destination.

Vision is what gives a team direction and an ultimate destination, a vivid mental picture of what they are aiming for and what success looks like. A great vision is a driving force that compels people to do something. It propels teams to go the extra mile, to aim high and push forward to create something that, perhaps, has not been done before.

I attended a training session early in my career where one of the exercises was to break up in teams and brainstorm as many ideas as we could for earning ten dollars. Everyone enthusiastically huddled in their teams and got to work on this fun assignment.

After 20 minutes or so, the instructor stopped us and asked for feedback from the audience on some of their ideas. There were some very innovative concepts, and every team had already come up with a substantial number of activities that could earn someone ten dollars in a day. We were all feeling pretty smug about our creativity and proud of our growing lists of ideas.

The instructor then asked if any of the ideas presented so far could earn someone a million dollars. People looked at their lists, and each other, and not surprisingly the consensus was that most of the ideas on our lists had absolutely no chance of making anyone a million dollars.

The instructor then made his point—"You don't get million-dollar ideas from a ten-dollar vision."

The instructor had asked us to shoot for ten-dollar ideas, so no one even thought about aiming higher than that. I've always thought that was such a clever way to help a team understand the importance of having a vision and aiming high—giving a team a big, bold, and clear target.

Creating a vision is one of the fundamental responsibilities of a leader, no matter what kind of work their team is doing. A vision isn't just something for a sales team, or a start-up team, or something to be developed at the department head or corporate level.

Regardless of the size team you lead, whether you lead 5 people or 50,000 people, a strong leader paints a very clear picture, creates a compelling rallying cause, that everyone can get behind and get excited about. It is a picture of what your organization could and should be.

At one time in my career, I was leading a team of people whose job it was to verify white pages listings data for publishing in telephone directories. This was tedious, monotonous work with little opportunity for anyone to shine and no opportunity to be creative or innovative. It's hard to think about how you would create a compelling and exciting vision for a team like this.

Remember the scene in the 1979 movie *The Jerk* that starred Steve Martin, where he runs out to the van delivering the local phone books, grabs the book from the delivery man's hands, and frantically searches for his name? All while yelling, "The new phonebooks are here; the new phonebooks are here... Page 73, I'm somebody now!"

That's the vision I wanted to create for the team—to be the telephone directory that people waited for, ran out to the van to grab so they could look up their name and see that they were somebody. I wanted us to be the directory that people couldn't wait to have delivered to their doorstep.

That may not sound exciting today, but in those days there were multiple phone directories that were delivered to people's doorsteps, and the one they chose to keep was the one that was most complete and accurate. That was also the directory that advertisers were most interested in placing their advertising in.

To achieve our vision of being the directory everyone waited for and wanted to keep, we had to deliver close to 100% accuracy, and as we improved accuracy and reduced errors we would be reducing costs for the corporation and contributing to growth in advertiser revenue.

So we used that scene from *The Jerk* as our rallying cry. In our minds we saw Steve Martin running for *our* directory. I would play that clip and we would have fun with it, and we would talk about what it would take for us to be *that* phone book. We got excited about how much of an impact we could actually have on our customers and our business.

We created a fun and compelling vision for a team doing monotonous, repetitive work hour after hour, day after day. They could envision what that success would look like, and the credit they would get for achieving that vision. They clearly understood that every one of the team members must engage to achieve it, and each of them understood the critical role that they personally could play in that success.

That vision was a rallying cause that the entire team could get excited about. It drove engagement, it drove action, and it drove results.

I firmly believe that you can create a compelling vision for any type of work or organization.

If you're leading a customer service organization that deals with customer complaints all day long, paint a picture for them of the role that they play in retaining customers, in delighting customers with the solutions they can offer and by recovering well from an error. Help them understand the critical role they play in setting the sales team up for success and ultimately driving revenue for the corporation.

Even if you're managing a part of the business where technology is changing the nature of people's jobs in the future, your role as a leader is to find a way to paint a picture of a future that keeps the team engaged. Get them focused on the development of their own skills and the chance to prepare for opportunities in other areas of the business. Help them get excited about their role in helping customers adopt emerging technology and be true pioneers who lead others into new realms of knowledge.

Big ideas get people excited. Create a vision that gives real meaning to people's work, that gives them a reason to be there every day and a reason to be excited about the work they do and the outcomes they can deliver. Give them something to shoot for, a lighthouse to constantly keep in their sight.

People want to feel motivated to come to work because what they do matters and makes a difference.

With a compelling vision you have a team who understands and believes in where you're trying to go. Now you have to create passion for that vision and constantly connect the work your team does every day to that vision.

2. CONNECT people to the vision

People have to have a deep belief that the work they do matters and makes an important contribution to the vision.

It's not enough to create a vision and stick it up on the wall. You have to connect the dots for people.

The vision is the *what* you want to achieve. Now you need to give your team the *why*—convince them that they have a vested interest in achieving it. And you have to bring the vision to life every day in a way that the team feels an *emotional connection* to it.

That requires three things:

1. Ensuring every individual feels that they personally play a key role in achieving the vision.
2. Helping your team understand the WIFM factor—What's In It For Me? They need to know what's in it for them if they go all-in to achieve the vision.
3. Constantly communicating the vision so that every person on your team knows it and can repeat it. It must be the force that guides their actions and decisions on a daily basis.

Your team needs to understand how what they do matters in the achievement of the overall vision. If your vision is too lofty, too far removed from what people do every day, it might be a great and exciting vision but it won't drive action or performance because they won't understand how they personally can make a difference. Test your vision in that way—make sure every person on your team sees themselves and their daily work as being critical to the achievement of the vision. You need everyone to feel that if they slack off, they are letting the whole team down and standing in the way of the team getting to the vision.

Once your team understands and believes their work is critical, you've got their buy-in. Now you need to create exciting *motivation* that energizes them to go all-in to achieve the vision. They need to know what's in it for them if they achieve it. They need to know how this will benefit them if the team is successful.

Will this streamline their future work? Are there financial incentives for them? Get the team excited about how achieving the vision will ultimately make their work more effortless, create more jobs, or lead to bonuses.

You also need to convey what will happen if the team doesn't achieve the vision. Will it lead to loss of jobs or reductions in pay? Don't spend a lot of time focusing on the negative aspects of missing the goals, but you do want members to understand there are consequences that will personally impact the team.

Think of ways the team will receive recognition if they achieve the vision. Will their name be in lights, forever tied to the success of the achievement? Will they be recognized publicly in front of their peers? Paint a picture of how their achievements will contribute to the overall success and growth of the company, the far-reaching benefits to its customers, how they will have accomplished something that will benefit all employees.

Be realistic, but get creative and make it so compelling that they cannot wait to get started on the journey to the desired destination.

Now that you've got them energized and motivated to go for it, you need to clearly and repeatedly communicate your organization's vision over and over and over again to maintain momentum and make sure the team always keeps the vision in sight.

There's a saying that its only when you tire of hearing yourself say it that people even begin to absorb it. Repeat it until you're tired of hearing it, and that's the point at which the team is just starting to get it.

Communicate in both small and big ways. Tie the day's events back to the vision to highlight the relevance of even the day-to-day work. Use internal memos, presentations, and posters to remind the team of their purpose and goals. Constantly use examples of how individual achievements are contributing to the vision.

Incorporate the vision in every presentation or written communication you send. Make it a part of the objective setting and performance review process. Include it in projects that cut across other departments. Keep it at the center of all that you do to focus your team and direct their efforts.

Your constant communications will keep people thinking and talking about that exciting picture you have created for them—the desired destination. Draw people toward the vision, like moths to a porch light. **The more a vision can be expressed in a vivid, imaginative way, the more it will motivate people to take action in the present.**

There are many great examples of companies who have created visions that paint a vivid picture for employees and get them excited about the incredible impact their work can have:

- To be the company that best understands the product, service, and self-fulfillment needs of women—globally. *Avon*
- To be the number one advocate in the world for human worth in organizations. *The Ken Blanchard Companies*
- A personal computer in every home running Microsoft software. *Microsoft Computers*
- To be the world's most customer-centric company. *Amazon*
- Making the best possible ice cream, in the nicest possible way. *Ben & Jerry's*

The leaders of these companies created compelling visions that drove action and guided decisions, and they constantly conveyed their visions through their words and actions so that all employees believed in it, understood their role in achieving it, and were willing to go all-in to make it happen.

There are many ways of communicating and connecting people to a vision. Following are some tips from John Kotter, creator of the 8-Step Process for Leading Change, concerning the third step: Form a Strategic Vision and Initiatives.

1. Keep the message simple and jargon-free. A vision should be something everyone can remember and repeat.
2. Use analogies and stories to paint a vivid picture for employees.
3. Repeat, repeat, repeat—ideas only sink in after they've been heard many times.
4. Refer to elements of the vision in every communication.
5. Constantly link behaviors, initiatives, and results to the vision.
6. Engage all levels of the organization in communicating the vision and bringing it to life. People learn and internalize most effectively by *doing* rather than by simply reading or listening.
7. Explain seeming inconsistencies—if you don't it undermines credibility and buy-in to the vision.
8. Allow for constant feedback and dialogue.

Walking the talk is also important in connecting people to the vision. As a leader of any team, you have to "bring it" every single day. The energy, passion, and commitment that you bring to the job is the energy, passion, and commitment that will be transmitted to your people. People want to follow a leader with passion, it makes them believe in the vision and the work. Always remember that people watch your actions, not just your words.

Now you have a vision that your team is excited about, and they clearly understand the role each of them plays in achieving it. They see that there are good things in store for them if they hit the goal. They hear you talking about it and living it out through your words and actions. You've drawn them in and they are ready and anxious to make it happen.

But they can't do it without out you, their coach, rolling up your sleeves and getting in the trenches to help your people be successful.

3. COACH people to success

Even the best players don't get better without a good coach.

One of the biggest frustrations I've experienced throughout my career is the fact that many leaders are poor coaches of their people. They know how to give direction and orders, but those things alone don't drive success. You have to be on the field with your team, constantly observing the play and providing coaching, feedback, and encouragement.

I've always struggled with why leaders so avidly avoid giving people feedback. Not good feedback, every leader is fairly proficient at giving a "You're doing a good job" in a performance review. But it seems to be so difficult for leaders to give constructive feedback. And every single person on your team has something they need to work on, something they can improve upon that will help them advance.

People need to hear about the areas they need to improve or they will never get better. Failing to give them that feedback is denying them the opportunity to grow and develop their skills. It is lulling them into a false sense that what they're doing is good enough—that they are succeeding in their current role and are doing what it takes to be ready for the next one.

Ken Blanchard says, "Feedback is the breakfast of champions." It is the sustenance your people need, on a regular basis, to learn and grow. You shouldn't wait for an annual performance review to sit down with people and give them feedback, you need to be giving it to them on an ongoing basis, no less than once a month. The underlying motivation for giving feedback is the belief that the recipient can do better, and feedback needs to be timely to be relevant and actionable.

Make sure your feedback is specific. Stick to the facts, don't make it personal, and don't let emotions get in the way of the message. Talk about what you observed and don't get into what you *think* happened. For example, you could say that the project you gave him wasn't completed on time, but don't put words in his mouth and tell him you think it's because he's not interested in his job. Focus instead on the impact of not having the project completed on time and how it affected others. Give him a chance to explain what happened, but don't accept excuses. Make your expectations clear, and offer your support if there are training, tools, or resources he needs.

When you give feedback, leave people with the understanding that you believe they are capable of improving and you are there to provide whatever support they need to make it happen.

As a leader, you owe every person on your team the constructive feedback they need to improve. It's a fundamental responsibility of leadership. And they *want* to improve, but they need your help in identifying how. Of course they want to be told what they're doing well, but they *also* want you to help identify where their weak spots are and how to shore them up so they can improve their overall performance.

Years ago I stepped into a role and acquired a new team of direct reports I hadn't worked with before. As I got to know them, one woman stood out as being a star—she was smart, poised, articulate, she always exceeded results and she was just all-around impressive. I'll call her Beverly.

One of the things I always do when I step into a new role is talk to others outside of my organization to get their input and feedback on the talent on my team. As I talked to other leaders, I was surprised that my peers had a negative opinion of Beverly—they said she was perceived as not being a team player, as always trying to outshine others and even elbow others out of the way to get credit. The feedback was pretty consistent, and my peers said this behavior had been going on for many, many years—and was so pervasive that others were unwilling to consider her for positions in their organizations. I was shocked that someone with so much potential was sabotaging her own career with this behavior. I scheduled time to sit down with Beverly and give her the feedback.

I first let her know how impressed I was with her command of the business, her communication skills, her ability to consistently deliver results. And then I let her know that as a way to get to know my team and understand strengths and opportunities, I had sought feedback from others outside of our organization about her. I told her that she was indeed perceived as smart, capable, and competent, but that others perceived her as not being a team player and it would prevent her from being considered for other opportunities. I gave her specific examples based on the feedback I had gotten from others.

She was totally taken aback by the feedback. She had been with the company for 15 years, in her current position for 2 years, and although everyone seemed to know her reputation, no one had ever given her that feedback. No one had ever given her a chance to fix it.

She said, "I've never understood why I was constantly rated as a top performer but I've felt that I wasn't being considered for promotion or even other lateral opportunities. No one ever told me there was something I needed to change."

It is completely irresponsible as a leader to know there are traits or skill gaps or even style issues that are holding one of your employees back and not give them that feedback. The absence of feedback sends the signal that they should keep doing what they are doing, and the travesty of enabling someone like Beverly to operate without constructive feedback for many years is that the behaviors are even more ingrained and harder to change over time.

I worked hard to help Beverly work on the behaviors she needed to change. I got her an executive coach who worked with her with some success. To her credit, she dug in and worked hard to change her behavior.

But it's hard to change a *reputation* after that many years of being perceived as not a team player. We had done her a real injustice by not giving her a chance to correct her behavior much earlier in her career.

To be a great leader you need to get in the trenches and truly coach your people, giving them the feedback they need to improve and the resources they need to make it happen. Spend time with each one to understand their strengths, weaknesses, and motivations. Set high expectations, hold people accountable, but then roll up your sleeves and get in there with them to give them the support they need to be successful.

A great coach creates an environment where everyone on the team has the tools and resources to do their jobs well, and they know they have the constant support of the leader. It becomes a healthy learning environment where the team pulls together to help each other. People want to come to work because they know that even when they're having a bad day the team will rally around them and help.

There is a tremendous amount of training available about how to be an effective coach or supervisor. Most companies have internal resources available to help new supervisors with the fundamentals of coaching, but there are a wide range of materials available publicly as well. Take advantage of every opportunity to learn good coaching habits and techniques early on;

the fundamentals of coaching are critical to success and to your ability to become a truly great leader.

You will have teams with a wide range of performers—from the top performers who are self-motivated and need very little coaching, to the bottom performers who most likely have a variety of needs. Don't make the mistake of just assuming that your lowest performers lack the skill to do the work.

At one time early in my career I stepped in to a role supervising a team of 14 people all doing the same type of work resolving customer issues. The leader I was replacing, as he was walking out the door to his new role, took me aside and gave me some "tips" about my new team. He said, "There are two top performers on this team, seven average performers, and the other five shouldn't be here. Focus on your top performers, that's what I do, I push them hard and they carry the team."

I couldn't believe it; it was wrong on so many levels.

1) His team wasn't meeting their overall objectives so why did he think he could just rely only on the performance of his top talent? Isn't that the definition of insanity—doing the same thing over and over again and expecting a different result? It wasn't working.

2) If he thought five of his employees shouldn't be there, why were they still there? What had he done to coach them up or out?

And 3) He was doing nothing to try to move some of his average players up to stronger performance. I couldn't help but think if he had been properly coaching his employees and managing performance his team's results might have looked vastly different.

I dug in with the team, first focusing on the low performers with the intent of either moving them up or out. I spent a little time getting to know each one, and I observed their work for a period of time every day. And I learned something very quickly. Each of the five had completely different challenges, and I believed if we could overcome those their performance would improve.

One of them simply lacked confidence. He was not confident in his ability to explain certain products to customers but was afraid to ask for help because he was already perceived as a poor performer. So his sales were low because he shied away from selling the products he lacked the ability to explain in a proficient way. Once we got him the training that he needed, and did some intense role playing, he was ready to step up and his performance immediately improved.

One of them had a husband who had recently been diagnosed with a serious illness and she was distracted and felt that no one at work cared or even knew about what she was struggling with. She needed some emotional support and a little time off. The team rallied to provide some meals at home and some extra encouragement and support at work, and after a brief leave of absence she came back ready to do her part to deliver results.

Another I found to be completely capable and incredibly smart, he just felt demotivated by all the attention the top sellers were getting, and the less recognition and coaching he got, the more he lost his will to perform. We put him in charge of a project for the team—gathering best practices from other teams on how to bundle our products and services. He did an outstanding job, received a lot of recognition and appreciation, and having led the best practice project he used what he learned to improve his own selling skills.

Yet another one was never going to be a star, but she needed some intense, ongoing side-by-side coaching, a little hand-holding and some ongoing encouragement and she was able to bring her performance up to an acceptable level.

My predecessor was right about only one of the five—there was in fact one person on the team who lacked both the skill and the will to be there. After working with him for about 30 days, we agreed that he was in the wrong spot and I helped him get to a position where his skills were a closer match for the work.

But the other four just needed help, support, understanding, and confidence. With good, solid coaching, each of them was able to improve their performance and be a solid, contributing member of the team.

The best managers get outstanding performance from ordinary human beings. If you wait for a team of superstars, you will be waiting forever.

You should never make assumptions and pigeonhole people as poor performers or good performers. Discover what each person does best. Bring people together to support and encourage each other. Believe 100% in your people, and you'll find they will rise to the level of your belief in them.

As the leader, engage one on one with your people and understand their skill, their weaknesses, and their motivations so you can effectively coach people to improved performance.

An interesting dynamic that occurred with my team of 14 was that as the 7 "average" performers saw me demonstrate genuine interest in the success of the team, believing in the low performers and coaching them to improved performance, their energy and engagement increased and their performance improved without any intense coaching efforts by me. The entire team rose to the level of my belief in them.

Good, healthy coaching and genuine care and concern for the team creates a dynamic that takes on a life of its own. It builds trust, creates an environment where the team works together and pulls together, and creates a team that people want to be a part of and do their part to succeed.

4. CHALLENGE the team to reach higher

Winning creates energy and keeps everyone in the game.

At this point you've created a vision that the team can rally around and is excited about. You have constantly communicated that vision to ensure that every single member of the team feels connected to it and understands the critical role they play in the achievement of that vision. You have gotten in the trenches with your people to provide strong coaching, giving them the tools, training, and resources they need to be successful.

Your work here isn't yet done, there are two more critical elements to driving teams to deliver results and achieve the goals.

Everyone loves to be a part of a winning team. And you as the leader play a critical role in setting the team up to achieve, and exceed, the goals and in making every member of the team feel the incredible energy that comes from being a contributor to a team that is winning.

Once you have the team rocking along and delivering results, your job is to *challenge* them to do even more.

Winning doesn't feel very rewarding when the goal is low... but when the goal is high and the team hits it, and then goes beyond it, wow does that create momentum.

So *aim high*, but make the goal achievable. If the target is out of reach and the team never gets enough momentum to even get close, they lay down before they start. An unattainable goal is demotivating, the opposite of what you're trying to achieve.

Set interim goals, milestones to shoot for and celebrate. When you hit those, celebrate, and then *aim higher.* That generates an energy that takes on a life of its own. Stay engaged with your team and keep cheering them on at every single milestone along the way, challenging them to strive for more.

When I was running operations for the publishing company, I had responsibility for all of our call center operations. The primary responsibility of our customer service reps was to take calls from customers who had complaints or concerns about their yellow pages ads in our printed directories. We held the reps primarily accountable for customer satisfaction, measured by customer surveys after the call.

Errors sometimes occurred in the production and printing process that resulted in the customer asking for a credit or adjustment on the cost of their ad. Errors ranged from the color in the printed directory ad not matching the advertiser's logo colors, to a transposed telephone number which would result in consumers not being able to call the advertiser. When a telephone number was incorrect, the ad was effectively useless to the advertiser, and we would often credit the entire amount of their advertising. When a logo color was off, we would negotiate with the customer and attempt to convince them that they were still getting an effective return on the cost of their advertising—the color of the logo would not prevent customers from calling. So there was a wide range of adjustments and credits that reps could negotiate with customers based on the nature of the error.

These credits and adjustments were a huge cost to the business, and when I dug into our annual adjusted revenue and did some external benchmarking, I realized our credits and adjustments were much higher than they should be.

We were giving more than 8% of our total revenue back to customers in the form of credits and adjustments. Benchmarking showed that our adjusted revenue should be closer to 5% to be average, and closer to 3% to be best in class.

It became apparent that the company had trained customers to get some or all of their money refunded. That if they called after their ad was printed they could pretty much always get some money back on their ad. We had created an unintentional "discount" program in our efforts to keep customers happy and drive customer satisfaction.

We had a long way to go to even get to average, but the savings to the corporation would be huge if we could get there so we set out to develop a plan.

The sales and ad creation process were where the errors were typically created, and they signed up to do their part to reduce errors. But customer service was the organization that took the calls from customers and negotiated the adjustments, so we knew we could have a significant impact on reducing adjusted revenue.

I worked with my direct report team to determine what progress we thought we could make by the end of the year in reducing adjusted revenue. I had high expectations, I told them going in to the discussion that I was not going to be satisfied with just getting to average. We agreed that our vision would be to get to best in class in credits and adjustments.

After much discussion, we agreed to a goal of cutting our adjustments in half by year-end, getting to 4%. We all were confident that if we could achieve that kind of progress in the current year, we would get to our vision of being best in class the following year.

Reducing credits and adjustments required that we refine and simplify our adjustment policy and re-train our customer service reps to re-sell the value of the ad rather than giving money back as a way to make advertisers happy. My team knew that this would be a big change for our reps, and they would have a lot of angst about their role in negotiating with customers to reduce adjustments.

We knew that if we communicated our goal of cutting adjustments in half in one year, the reps would be overwhelmed with the huge target and we would have a tough time making them believe we could get there. So we decided that instead of communicating the year-end target, we would set quarterly milestone targets, increasing the target each month as we made progress, driving to 4% by the end of the year.

We started small so we could give them an achievable target and a big win in the first quarter to build confidence and generate excitement and momentum. We gave them a goal of reducing adjustments by just 1% for that quarter. That might sound underwhelming, but it would require that they give millions of dollars less in adjustments to customers in that quarter. So to the reps it felt like a big target, but the leadership team all knew it was completely attainable with standardization of our credit policy, retraining of reps, and good coaching to help reps get comfortable with our new policy and negotiation process.

It took a tremendous amount of effort on the part of the leadership team to communicate our vision of getting to best in class in adjustments, to get their teams on board, and to do the training and coaching required to change behavior and give reps the confidence they needed to stand firm when there was no real error in an ad.

But we did it, in that first quarter we beat our target. It was a very small step toward our larger vision of getting to best in class but it was a really important milestone for the team.

We had a huge celebration to recognize what the team had accomplished. We highlighted top performers who had already succeeded in reducing their credits and adjustments to 3% to show the rest of the team what was possible. We let those reps share their tips and best practices with the rest of the team.

At that celebration, we capitalized on the excitement and energy of the moment to let the team know we thought we could do even better, we *aimed higher* and we communicated our target for the second quarter. We talked about the celebration we would have when we reached that target. And we called on reps to tell the team what they were going to do to continue to reduce their credits and adjustments—getting them excited about and invested in continuing to drive improvements. The team was so jazzed by their accomplishment and the recognition they had received that they were ready to tackle the bigger objective and determined to exceed their goal again in the second quarter.

The team executed in an amazing way throughout the balance of the year, and by year-end they had exceeded their target and were close to getting to our best in class vision. We achieved our vision in the first quarter of the next year.

If we had simply told the team that our expectation was to cut adjustments in half in one year, it would have been difficult to get them excited and on board. Giving them interim milestones to hit, celebrating in a big way, and then aiming higher got everyone excited and in the game in a way that allowed us to achieve even more than we thought possible.

Challenging your team isn't the same thing as being a cheerleader. You can't just say "Great job, I know you can deliver 10% more" without being specific about exactly what your team can do to deliver that 10% more. So you have to know your team and know your numbers, know where and how far to push and know where to be more conservative.

One of the most effective motivators for a team is giving them something fun to look forward to when they achieve a milestone or a goal. It doesn't have to be a big or expensive thing, it can simply be something fun that motivates the team to work harder, perform better and win.

When I was running sales call centers at one point later in my career, we constantly ran monthly contests to drive performance. There were a number of fun things we offered to the winning center each month.

We offered to have the entire leadership team come and put on aprons and chefs hats and grill burgers and hot dogs, outside in the hot sun, and then serve them to the winning team. We offered an afternoon ice cream social, with sundaes and banana splits dipped up by the big boss. We offered full days of mentoring sessions with senior leaders. We even paid off one contest by having senior leaders sit in a dunking booth in the parking lot and get dunked all day. If I remember correctly, that contest generated one of our highest grossing months ever!

Challenge your team, keep spurring them on in fun and creative ways as they hit interim targets and milestones, give them the credit, and they will achieve things you never thought possible.

5. CELEBRATE...give credit and recognition freely

What motivates people is the feeling of being seen and recognized, of being part of a team. People will give their time for a paycheck, but they will give a piece of their lives for meaningful work.

As the leader, you have created a vision, connected people to that vision, coached them individually to enable them to succeed, and you have challenged them to do more, aim higher, and achieve more than they ever thought possible. You've created incredible momentum and excitement and the team has achieved in a way they never dreamed they could.

Imagine, at this point, how your team would feel if you failed to recognize or celebrate that success. If they exceeded all their goals and were met with nothing but silence—chirping crickets rather than the blaring trumpets and cheering crowds they expected. Their momentum would hit a brick wall and they would ultimately feel that all that hard work went unrecognized and unrewarded.

It would be like getting to the finish line in a marathon and having no ribbon to break through, no cheering crowd to recognize the incredible accomplishment. It would be like a cast performing a hit play on a Broadway stage and at the end of the play the audience just sits in silence and then slowly gets up and leaves. Where is the feedback and recognition for the performance? Where is the celebration and applause they deserve? Where is the incentive to come back and do it again the next night?

The celebration of the victory—appreciation, thanks, recognition—is just as important a part of leadership as the drive to get there. The more you praise and celebrate success, the more people are motived to achieve. We all want to feel like winners whose contributions and results are noticed and appreciated.

I've reviewed hundreds of employee surveys and feedback tools over the years, and never once has an employee said, "I wish they would stop all this recognition, it's way too much!"

Sincere thanks never grow old. Ongoing, meaningful rewards and recognition are critical elements of building morale, creating energy and maintaining excitement, and encouraging teams to go the extra mile to deliver extraordinary performance. At the end of the day, people always want to feel that they made a difference, that they contributed to the team in some way.

Celebrate the team's accomplishments in ways that engage and energize the entire team—group lunches, recognition dinners. Even simple and inexpensive celebrations like having a pajama day or a team spirit day where employees can wear their favorite team's jerseys creates some fun at work and can be a great motivator for a team.

I've seen leaders come up with incredibly creative ways to recognize team members that cost very little money and pay very big dividends. Following are some examples:

1. Send a hand-written thank you note. *Never underestimate the impact of a hand-written note.* I have employees who have kept notes leaders have written them on the walls of their cubicle for years.
2. Post a thank you note on an employee's cubicle or door so their co-workers can see it.

3. Give special assignments to people who show initiative.
4. Arrange for a team to present the results of its efforts to upper management. This is not only recognition for them, but a learning and growth opportunity as well.
5. Encourage and recognize employees who pursue continuing education.
6. Establish a place to display memos, posters, photos that recognize individual employees for achievements, or progress toward goals.
7. Swap a task with an employee for a day—his/her choice. Let an employee shadow you for the day.
8. Establish a "Behind the Scenes" award specifically for those whose actions are not usually in the limelight. Don't just recognize those who are always in the spotlight.
9. Present "State of the Department" reports periodically to your employees, publicly acknowledging the work and contributions of individuals and teams.
10. At a monthly staff meeting, award an Employee of the Month and invite co-workers at the meeting to say why that person is deserving of the award.
11. Recognize employees who actively serve the community, or who lead the charge for health and wellness in the office. Recognition doesn't have to just be about the top performers or superhuman efforts; it is motivating to recognize others for their unique contributions as well. Even the smallest recognition matters deeply to people.

12. Have the team vote for top manager, supervisor, employee and rookie of the year. Recognition by your peers is powerful.
13. Name a continuing recognition award after an outstanding employee.
14. Allow employees to attend meetings in your place when you are not available.
15. Designate a special parking spot for the "Employee of the Month." The criteria can be changed periodically based on the behavior you are trying to incentivize.

Thomas Jefferson, third President of the United States, once said, "The glow of one warm thought is worth more to me than money."

Celebration and recognition matter.

So those are my 5 C's of Leadership, how to put your leadership skills to work driving results:

- CREATE a vision
- CONNECT people to the vision
- COACH people to success
- CHALLENGE the team to deliver even more
- CELEBRATE…give credit and recognition freely

A great leader makes all the difference in the performance of a team. A team with a great leader understands exactly what they are being asked to do and why, and they are bought in. They can visualize the end goal and they are jazzed and motivated by it. They know precisely what they can and must do as a team and as individuals to achieve the goals. They have the tools and resources to do their jobs well and the constant support of the leader when they need help. They are excited about the reward that awaits when they meet their goals. They feel appreciated and respected, as team members and as *people*, and they work so closely as a unit that it begins to feel like a family. They want to come to work every day because they are a collaborative group of individuals with a shared purpose, and even when they're having a bad day they know they will be lifted up by their team. They love what they do because it feels good to be part of a winning team.

Be a 5 C's leader who drives results.

Chapter 8: Debbie's Double Dares

I've shared the highs and lows of my leadership journey with you, and I've used my experiences to highlight for you many of the lessons I've learned in my 34-year career journey. I hope the stories and examples have brought those lessons and insights to life for you in a way that inspires you and gives you courage to dream big and the confidence to believe that you can achieve your version of success.

Up to this point, I've been *sharing* with you.

Now I want to *challenge* you, to *dare* you. Think of the following four challenges as Debbie's Double Dares.

1. I dare you to be yourself, be authentic, be true to who you are.

It has always surprised me how many leaders attempt to be one way at work and believe their "true" personality can only emerge outside of work. And those same leaders are surprised when their employees are uncomfortable with them—don't completely trust them, don't like them, and don't feel they can be themselves around them.

Authentic leadership is showing your real self to your followers. No human being is a perfectly formed work of art, and neither are you. Authenticity is not being afraid to show who you are, with your genuine strengths and human frailties.

Authentic leaders lead with their hearts and their minds. They are not afraid to show emotion, and they connect with their employees by allowing their passion to shine. Authentic leaders have unfailing integrity, allowing them to instill complete trust in their people and lead through influence rather than position power.

I've seen so many women struggle, as they rise through the ranks, to fit into the mold of the "executive" image they think they are expected to portray. And in my observation, it causes stress for the woman and causes her to lose credibility with her team as she becomes less authentic and more, well, almost robotic. It creates distance between her and her team.

Don't make the mistake of believing you have to pretend to be someone you're not. There is no "mold" you need to make yourself fit into.

Do you need to be conscious of the image you portray? Yes. Do you need to develop executive presence? Absolutely. But that doesn't mean you stop being you.

When women ask me about executive presence, wondering what it means and if they have to become some unnatural version of themselves to achieve it, I say absolutely not.

Executive presence is about being *relatable* to your audience, being someone who commands respect, being confident and poised under pressure, and being decisive. It's not about looking a certain way; it's more about maintaining your personal style but not making *mistakes* in appearance that are so distracting that the audience is unable to relate to you or to focus on your message. I mean skirts that are too short, blouses that are too low-cut or provocative, or hair that is unkempt. Those things can be so distracting that it prevents others from being able to get past them to see what's on the inside.

At various times in my career I've had to give feedback to someone whose appearance or presence was preventing people from seeing them as a professional. And I've always told them—dress for the position you want, not the one you have.

People have to be able to envision you in a bigger role, picture you standing in front of a big team or meeting with customers or talking with investors. If your appearance is less than professional, or worse—distracting—it's tough for people to see you in those roles.

If you aspire to be in a role with regular contact with major customers, and your leaders only see you in the office every day in jeans and a t-shirt, it is hard for them to envision you holding a professional meeting with a big customer.

Maybe we wish it didn't matter, but it does. Because you have to *earn* your reputation and the right to do more and to advance.

Once you have demonstrated what you're capable of doing, and you have established your reputation and your personal brand, your edginess or quirkiness can come out more and you don't risk being misunderstood or unrelatable. So don't give up what makes you, but make sure you are relatable and that people can envision you in the role you want to achieve.

At the other end of the spectrum is the mistake many women make of thinking they need to fit the "image" that is expected of them, particularly as they rise into increasing positions of authority.

Lisa was a woman in our company who was incredibly talented, very well-respected and well-liked, who had risen very rapidly through the ranks of the company. She was a little quirky, she definitely had her own style, but she had earned a reputation and it didn't matter what she wore or how casually she spoke—people knew her immense capabilities and talent and when she spoke people listened intently and related deeply to the message. Her people loved her and related to her.

Until Lisa was promoted into a big new role with a lot of visibility, and she began to become someone she wasn't. In this new position, Lisa felt that she was expected to be more polished, more "corporate," and that she couldn't afford to be as casual and relaxed as she had been in the past.

Lisa began to try to morph into the image she thought she needed to uphold. Her unique style of communicating that had worked so well was replaced with a much more buttoned-up style. She used notes and memorized speeches rather than talking passionately and personally with her audience.

It actually became painful to watch her on stage as she worked to evolve into this new polished image. With each successive meeting it got worse as she got more nervous and became more uncomfortable, and you could actually see her shaking on stage as she tried to fake a style that wasn't natural to her. Some of her team were actually embarrassed for her—this wasn't the confident, personable Lisa they knew. She wasn't reaching her audiences and her discomfort began to detract from her message.

It is exhausting wearing a mask, trying to be someone you're not.

I can't say that I know exactly the thought process that went through Lisa's head during this time, but I watched the results unfold. Maybe she realized that not only was this "mold" she had poured herself into uncomfortable for her, it was causing her to erode the wonderful connection she had had with her people. Maybe someone close to her gave her some coaching. Maybe she just got tired of the act and the stress and said to herself, "I have to go back to being me."

Whatever the reason, she stopped trying to be someone else, and it was a beautiful thing to watch.

She loosened up and began to relax and go back to the style that worked for her, in all her casual quirkiness. She stopped relying on notes and began speaking from the heart, with personality and passion. She was once again relatable to her audience.

She was not a naturally gifted speaker, and she didn't naturally project a buttoned-up and polished image, but her team related to a leader who was willing to be her authentic self, just be who she was, with all her incredible intelligence and talent and all her quirks and human frailties.

She is today a tremendously successful leader whose star will likely continue rising right to the top.

I went through something very similar at a point in my career when I was experienced enough to know better.

I had become known as a pretty good public speaker over the years. The public speaking course I had taken early in my career, coupled with years of being in positions that required me to stand in front of large audiences and deliver speeches and presentations, had given me enough practice and confidence that I actually loved standing on a stage and delivering a message with passion and energy.

I didn't typically use notes. I had learned over time that I was truly at my best when I knew my stuff and spoke from the heart. I seemed to be able to genuinely connect with an audience and convey a message in a way that people could not only understand and relate to it, but be excited about it.

But at one point I found myself in the position of having to present to the CEO and his leadership team on a variety of topics.

Now I had stood on stages and looked out at audiences of more than 2000 people. I had delivered presentations at the United Nations, in front of press corps in Washington, D.C, on stages in New York. I had done radio interviews with large listening audiences. I had delivered webcasts that were watched by thousands and thousands of people.

Nothing intimidated me more than presenting to this small group of leaders in an executive conference room. And I was seasoned enough to know better.

The first time I was scheduled to present to them, I did all the appropriate preparation that I would normally do—I created a terrific, crisp presentation, I reviewed it with my boss to ensure the material was right on point, I rehearsed in my head to ensure I knew the material backwards and forward.

I did the math calculations on every single number to ensure I could address any questions. I anticipated every question they might ask, and I made sure that I had all the back-up material I might need to answer them. I was absolutely, fully prepared and should have nailed that meeting.

But as the meeting approached I got nervous. I fell into the trap of thinking that I was now expected to present a different image here, that it wasn't appropriate to just be myself and speak from the heart. I thought I needed to be more professional, more buttoned up and crisp. It certainly didn't help that I knew I had 15 minutes on the agenda and I was well aware that running over my time would not be well-received.

So in the 24 hours before the meeting I did something I never typically did. I made notes. All over every page. I made notes of exactly what I wanted to say and how I wanted to say it. I wrote out my introduction, my transitions sentences between slides, my conclusion and closing. I wanted to make sure I didn't falter or pause at any point. I thought I would sound more confident and competent if I could just flawlessly read those notes and make it through the presentation that way.

Boy was I wrong. I read my notes all right, which kept me looking down at my presentation and not connecting at all with the leaders in the room. I stuck to my "script," and they heard the words, but I didn't let them see the passion and conviction I had about what I was saying. And I have no idea what the body language in the room was—you can't see body language when you're squinting at your own hand-written notes.

I finished on time, and I achieved what I needed to—they got the message and I got the outcome I was looking for. But let's just say I didn't impress anyone in that room that day. Because I wasn't being me. My presentation was nervous, rote, and fairly underwhelming.

I learned the lesson firsthand that day and I never made that mistake again.

The *real* you is always better than the *fake* you.

I've seen that play out time and again with people doing presentations, people at every single level of leadership. A presentation is *always* better, and an audience is always more engaged, when the speaker is being authentic and natural, just being who they are and conveying a message they are passionate about. It is also, by the way, one of the best ways not to be overly nervous—if you know all you need to do is be extremely well-prepared, and then just be you.

Your leadership style and your speaking style will absolutely evolve over time, and they should. And you have to deliberately work to be relatable to every audience you are trying to reach.

But don't change the core of who you are, what makes you YOU, to fit some mold.

You've heard the phrase "fake it till you make it"? That's about faking confidence, which we all have to do to overcome fear. But never, ever fake who you are.

I dare you to be authentic, be You.

2. I dare you to stop being a perfectionist.

Perfectionism is something that affects many high-achievers today, but women have a greater tendency than men to be perfectionists. We take such pride in our work, take it so personally, that even mild criticism stings. We want so desperately for our email messages to have just the right tone that it takes forever to hit send. We keep working so hard to complete tasks to our satisfaction that nothing ever feels finished. "Good enough" is never good enough for us.

We don't just strive for excellence—we believe we have to do everything to 100%, to perfection. We set an impossibly high standard for ourselves, determined to be the perfect employee, the perfect housekeeper, the perfect partner, the perfect mother, the perfect cook. The problem is that no matter how much we may want it to be so, perfection is not achievable, and the need to be perfect leaves us overworked, disappointed, and sometimes even immobilized.

That need to be perfect holds us back from answering a question, applying for a new job, asking for a raise, until we're *almost 100 percent sure* we can predict the outcome and avoid failure.

It causes us take on more than our share. Even when our plate is overloaded, we always step up when others fail to step in. And then we don't stop until we get an "A" in all of it.

There's a saying that if you chase two rabbits, both of them will get away. We're chasing a whole colony of rabbits every day, running ourselves ragged and stressing ourselves out, and many of those rabbits are getting away from us.

We can't keep that up; something has to give.

The drive to get everything to our ideal finished state, is a time drain, an energy sapper, and a confidence killer.

I dare you to accept that 80% of the time, 80% is good enough.

I'm not talking about being ill-prepared or doing a sloppy job.

I'm talking about making the best use of your time and energy by stopping at 80% on most things that you do so you can move on to the next thing on your list. There are clearly some tasks in life and work that warrant the additional effort to get to perfect, but at the end of the day, 80% is good enough on most things, and it's even perceived by others to be 100%.

Let's explore what happens when you don't stop at 80%, but continue to pour energy and brain power into getting everything to 100% perfect.

For any project, at work or at home, when you jump in and get it done, the first attempt is typically about 80% done. But you, the perfectionist, look at your presentation or project and you say to yourself, "I can do better."

So you continue working to get it the extra 20% complete. The problems with this are:

- 80% was probably good enough to begin with. You could have stopped there and everyone else around you would have felt the project was complete. Our 80% looks like 100% to everyone else. It just isn't good enough for you.
- The additional time it takes to get a project to 100% typically takes *more* time, causes more frustration, and has a much lower return for our efforts than the first 80%. "The Plateau Effect" is that critical inflection point, "the moment at which continued efforts produce little or no added benefit."
- Being a perfectionist, you never actually get to 100%, so you will keep going and tweaking, keeping yourself from moving on to the next project. So while you're spending additional effort on this project with no real return, all your other projects stack up in front of you.

At one point in my career I was leading a sales organization and the Chief Marketing Officer for the company was a brilliant and talented woman, I'll call her Doris. She had tremendous industry experience, she was smart, energetic, a driver of results. But she was a perfectionist who drained the energy from the room with her need to get everything to 100% perfection.

Doris frequently had to deliver presentations on our marketing strategy to the organization or our outside investors. Every single person on Doris's team dreaded the process of preparing her presentations and then working with her on rehearsing. Because they knew that the changes and tweaking never, ever stopped until Doris finally stepped on stage to deliver the presentation.

Doris's staff would spend days, often over weekends, putting together her presentation. Doris was engaged at every step along the way, looking at slides as they were created, making changes, changing her mind about how she wanted to talk about or characterize something. She paralyzed her staff—they couldn't get an entire presentation put together because they were constantly being re-directed by the changes Doris was making to the already completed slides. This was debilitating to the team, stifling creativity and sapping energy.

Doris would be engaged around the clock; time didn't matter to her. If she reviewed a version of the slides at 5 p.m. and directed changes, she expected to see a new draft that evening. It was the same over the weekend.

Once the team finally got an entire version of the deck completed and the meeting was approaching, Doris began rehearsing. Being a perfectionist, she insisted on rehearsing by going through the entire presentation just as she would give it, with her entire staff as the audience to help her perfect it. These "rehearsals" took place daily, at night, and on weekends, in the week leading up to a presentation, keeping her staff working almost around the clock.

With each rehearsal, Doris would find things she needed to change to get it to 100% perfect. She would dictate her changes and leave her staff at the office working on the next version, but she would check in repeatedly from home to ensure things were progressing as she thought they should.

This would go on until she stepped on stage, and every single time, Doris delivered an exceptional, brilliant performance.

However, it was never good enough for her, so after a presentation was complete she began the "debrief" process with her team, talking about what they, and she, needed to do differently to improve in the future.

After one of these presentations, Doris' staff decided to take a look at the first full presentation draft they had completed before Doris started tweaking and making changes, the 80% draft, and compare that to the final version that Doris presented. They realized that there were not really any material changes from their draft to the version Doris presented—the substance, data, and critical points of the presentation were all the same. The changes that took the team weeks of long hours and weekend work were not significant--words and phrases were tweaked, charts and text boxes were moved from one place on the slide to another, graphics were changed, and slides were shifted around. But the message was fundamentally the same, and would have been considered 100% complete and brilliantly delivered had Doris simply presented the first draft the team had delivered.

This is precisely the 80% concept. The amount of time it took the team to get to 80% was *half* the time it took to manage the other 20% that Doris imposed to get it to her version of perfect.

During the 20% time, the team had to set aside other work, wasting time on the 20% that delivered no material return.

The process sapped creativity, Doris' and the team's; it took time away from other valuable work; and it created an environment that deflated energy. Not surprisingly, people found it very stressful working for Doris

There are certainly times, and projects, that will warrant the extra time and energy to get something to 100%. Prioritize, and dedicate the time you need to those projects.

But for 80% of the work you do, remember that 80% is good enough.

Let go of the guilt, be willing to ask for help, and be willing to accept that some of the less-critical things won't get done the way you would like.

Know what really matters, and focus your creativity, energy, and time there.

I dare you to keep your life in balance and perspective and give up the need to be perfect.

3. I dare you to pursue your passion.

Life is too short to invest time in the things you aren't passionate about. In the course of a lifetime there are many things that will catch your eye, but only a few will capture your heart. Pursue those.

I believe God gives every one of us a gift, and if you can find it, hone it, and maximize it you will be on the road to living a life of passion and purpose.

Dare Number 3 is especially important to me because I'm blessed that I was able to have a 34-year career doing work that I loved and was passionate about.

I didn't love every single job, or every single boss I had over my career. But every single day I woke up excited about the opportunity to be the kind of leader that makes a difference for people.

When I was working for BellSouth in the 1990s, I had an executive coach who worked with me and other executives as part of our development activities to prepare for advancement in the company. My coach gave me a plaque that I have hanging on my wall to this day. The title is Master in the Art of Living, and it says:

> *"The Master in the art of living makes little distinction between his work and his play, his labor and his leisure, his mind and his body, his education and his recreation, his love and his religion. He hardly knows which is which. He simply pursues*

> *his vision of excellence in whatever he does, leaving others to decide whether he is working or playing. To him he is always doing both."* Ancient Chinese Proverb

Confucius said, "Do what you love and you'll never work a day in your life." It's great advice, but it's not always that simple—it can be difficult to figure out what you love and how to turn that into a viable business or a job. But it is possible, and it's worth it.

Early in my career, I could not have told you what my passion was. When I started working for the printing company right after college, I truly loved my job. Printing wasn't my passion, but I loved the opportunity to learn, to take processes apart and put them back together in a more effective way, to remove obstacles and make work more efficient for people.

When I moved to the publishing company, I didn't wake up every morning with a spring in my step because I was passionate about publishing, I woke up every morning looking forward to making a difference in the business, and for people. I loved helping people develop confidence, grow and learn, and feel that they were part of a winning team. I loved helping others find their passion in their work. And I loved the business results that were always the outcome of effective and caring leadership.

What gave me the greatest pleasure and satisfaction across all of the many roles I had over 34 years was having someone tell me that I made a difference in their work, their confidence, their career, their life.

And that's what I feel I was able to do throughout my entire career—make a difference for people. Sure I focused on constantly learning new parts of the business, on driving results, on driving change, on reducing costs and increasing sales. Those things were a part of my responsibility as a leader and I truly loved them, they gave me tremendous joy and pride.

But my passion was the people.

I've often been asked how you figure out your life purpose, how you determine what your passion is.

One suggestion I always give people is to periodically sit down and ask yourself the following questions and then write down the answers and come back to them over and over again:

1. What would you do if there was no risk of failure? What would you do if you were not afraid?
2. If money was not important, would you continue to work at the job you have or would you do something different?
3. What did you love as a child? Sometimes the pressures of growing up and earning a living squelch the things we naturally love and gravitate to.
4. Who is your professional hero?
5. What do you love doing outside of work? Where do you volunteer? What gives you the most pleasure?
6. If your life was absolutely perfect, what would that look like?

I believe it takes time to figure it out. You can't just sit down and write it up like you write a business plan and voila—you've identified your passion and purpose. You have to take steps, take *action*, and the more you act the more you will become clear on what you are passionate about and what you find draining and tiring.

With each step, the next one becomes more clear, but you have to be willing to reflect and listen to your heart.

Don't allow your passions to end up on the list of "maybe someday." And don't blindly continue to do the things that drain your energy and make you dread getting up in the morning. Be deliberate about honing in on your passion and using the unique gift God gave you, and you can achieve great things.

Nothing is more fun than to do what you love, love what you do, and feel like it matters.

I'm going to end this chapter with my fourth and final dare, and this is the dare that is closest to my heart. I'm giving you fair warning that I'm going to share some personal experiences here to show you the importance of attitude and resilience, and that there is more to life, and success, than luck.

4. I dare you to take responsibility for your attitude, because life is 10% what happens to us, and 90% how we respond to it.

We all have a choice, every day. We can choose an inner dialogue of self-encouragement and self-motivation, or we can choose one of self-defeat and self-pity. It's a power we all have. Each of us will encounter hard times, hurt feelings, heartache, loss, and physical and emotional pain over the course of a lifetime. The key is to realize it's not what happens to you that matters; it's how you choose to respond. You can choose to let circumstances defeat you, or you can choose to rise from the pain, stronger than before, and treasure the most precious gift you have—life.

> *"Man's rise or fall, success or failure, happiness or unhappiness depends on his attitude...a man's attitude will create the situation he imagines."* James Lane Allen, American novelist and short story writer

Few people ever sail through life or a career with smooth seas and strong tailwinds all along the way. The strongest and most successful are those who have faced adversity and come out the other side, tougher, wiser and more resilient than ever.

As you've heard in these pages, my career definitely hasn't been without its share of obstacles and curveballs. But not only have I faced curveballs professionally, I faced significant adversity in my personal life as well.

When I became pregnant with my son, it was the mid '80s and a time when many companies didn't have a maternity leave policy. Mine was one of those.

I had no idea how my boss or the company would react to my news. I didn't know of any women in the company who had left to have a baby and come back to work, so I had no precedent or role model. I was scared to death that as soon as I told them I was pregnant they might tell me they would have to replace me.

I waited until I was five months pregnant to let anyone in the company know, when I could no longer hide my growing belly. I continued to work through my entire pregnancy. I didn't want to give them any reason to feel I was shirking my duties. In fact, I worked until two weeks after my due date and finally experienced the first contractions that night, so the first day of work I missed was the day I went to the hospital in labor.

The entire time I was out after the birth of my son I still wasn't certain I would have a job to come back to. I kept in touch with my boss and my team, and the work, while I was out to ensure they knew I was still engaged at work. Every week I felt a little more relieved when no one gave an indication that I was being replaced. I was afraid to ask and give them any ideas, so I just held my breath and moved forward on the assumption that I still had a job.

I was so worried I might lose my job that when my son was four weeks old I asked my mom to come stay with him for a day so I could go in to the office and remind them I was still working and was still committed to the team and the company.

I came back to work full time after six weeks off to find that I still had an office, and a job. I had no idea whether I would be paid for any of that time off; I had not received a paycheck the entire time I was out. But a week after I returned to work I received a check for 50% of my pay for those six weeks. I felt very lucky to get that. And I believe the company developed a maternity policy after their experience with me to eliminate the ambiguity for other women who wanted to take maternity leave and return to work.

So it wasn't easy being a woman in management in that environment and I fought through a lot of obstacles to stay on the career path I knew I wanted and had earned.

There were other, more serious obstacles.

I woke up from an exploratory surgery when I was 40 years old to the voices of two surgeons rejoicing and saying, "We got it all!" All what?? Were they talking about me?

I had been having some intermittent abdominal pain and after a multitude of tests were inconclusive, my doctor decided exploratory surgery was the next step. As they wheeled me into surgery that morning, they had told my family that I should be back in the recovery room within an hour.

Seven hours later I was waking up to the sound of the surgeons' voices.

They told me they had opened me up and found cancer. Colon cancer. A very large colon cancer tumor. But we got it. In my groggy state I couldn't even comprehend what they were trying to tell me, and I drifted back into a restless sleep.

I later learned that they had opened me up to find that a large tumor had started in the colon and then entered my abdomen and was entangled in most of my abdominal organs. The tumor was everywhere, and they weren't sure how they could disentangle and remove it, but they decided that trying was the right path forward.

They went out to talk with my family and give them the news, and the options. They could operate and remove everything—that would require a significantly complex surgery, including a hysterectomy. Or they could attempt to remove only the tumor and leave me with the potential of having more children, but with the possibility that they couldn't get all of the cancer out.

My family said, "Save her life, get everything out that you can." I'm forever grateful that's the answer they gave.

It took over six hours of surgery, but the words "We got it all" were an incredible blessing for everyone to hear.

But there was one more diagnosis I was waiting to hear—the results of the lab tests. They had removed lymph nodes that would be tested to see if the cancer had spread, and it would take seven days for those results to come back.

As I recovered in my hospital room, surrounded by family and friends, I processed the fact that I had cancer. Cancer that was everywhere, all throughout my abdomen.

At that age, I didn't know many people who had had cancer. We didn't have a history of cancer in our family. I had definitely never heard of anyone who had a cancer tumor that had gotten loose and spread throughout organs who had survived.

I'm a fairly practical realist, and I faced the fact that it was likely they would find cancer in my lymph nodes. In fact, I believed it was possible that I might never leave the hospital.

I spent that week focused on preparing my family for that possibility. My son was 12 at the time, and I made sure he knew that if anything ever happened to me, my sisters and parents would take care of him and he would have an amazing life. I spent time ensuring my family knew how they would take care of him.

When the lab tests came back, the oncologist came to meet with me. I thought, This is it, this is where I learn whether I will survive this or not.

I still consider it a miracle, the work of God, that there was no cancer in my lymph nodes.

I asked about chemo, and the oncologist told me it was really my choice. If they had found cancer cells in the lymph nodes it would definitely have been the path forward, but I had the choice.

I didn't spend a minute debating it. I said, "If there is a chance that one cancer cell lingered I want to go get it. I want to have chemo." I started chemo several weeks later, after my strength returned enough for me to manage it. Six months of chemo, a three-hour infusion once a week.

The oncologist recommended that I do the infusion on Fridays, so that I could take the weekend to feel sick, recover, and feel better by the time I went back to work on Mondays.

I had a different idea. I said I want my infusions on Monday mornings. Being at work will keep my mind off of feeling sick, and then I can enjoy my weekends and my time with my family.

So every Monday I sat in that chair for three hours while the chemo dripped into my veins, and then I got on a plane and flew to wherever I needed to be that week. Monday night was always the worst night, and throughout the rest of the week I would gradually feel better. By the weekend I was almost back to normal again.

The treatment for colon cancer is not as toxic as some others so I was blessed that I never lost my hair, and that I was able to work throughout the six months of my treatment.

Quite a curveball I experienced, at 40 years old. All these years later, I am still cancer free.

But battling cancer was still not the most significant adversity I have faced in my life.

I have lived through the unbearable tragedy of losing my only son, Chad, the son I have talked about throughout this book, to suicide when he was 25 years old. The most important thing in my life, the son I loved and cherished and was so incredibly proud of, the motivation for everything I did.

It was an unimaginable shock; it was completely devastating. He was an amazing human being, with an inner light that lit up a room, and I was always so proud of him. He was warm, smart, funny, and the kindest and most accepting person I've ever known. He was the kind of young man that made all of my friends say, "How did you raise a child like that, I want my son to be just like him." At 25, he was one of my best friends.

I was always the person who watched the news, watched mothers who were talking about the terrible loss of a child, and thought, "I could never live through that. I don't know how any mother could ever survive the loss of their child."

I almost didn't survive it when it happened to me.

I learned that the body seems to have its own way of getting through a tragedy of this magnitude. Your brain seems to go into a sort of numb state. I went into a kind of shock, I constantly felt that there was a curtain between my brain and the outside world, a sheer curtain that I could see through but it muted everything that was going on around me.

I took some time away from work, but I couldn't bear the silence of my own thoughts, and the constant unbearable grief I felt was threatening to take me under.

So I went back to work, but I was on autopilot for a very long time. I had to put one foot in front of the other, every minute, every day, to keep going. I was afraid if I stopped for a minute the grief would overtake me and I would just lie down and never get up again.

My family, friends and co-workers surrounded me with love and support during this horrible time. I don't believe I would have found the courage to go on without them.

I also focused on my faith—I read every book I could find on suicide, surviving suicide, losing a child, life after death. I had to reground myself in my faith and what I believed. I had to try to understand the terrible depression and pain someone must feel to believe that death is the only way to find peace.

I learned so much about depression, that anyone can be affected despite their level of success or their place in life. People struggling with depression can be living a normal life on the outside—successful, loved, respected—while they are dealing with only darkness and torment on the inside. In fact, there is a good chance someone you know is struggling with it, since nearly 20% of American adults face some form of depression or mental illness in their lifetime.

There is nothing weak about a person struggling with depression. It takes incredible strength to keep pushing on when your brain is telling you that you are alone, no one feels like you do or even understands, you are a burden to others, you are a failure.

Because of the wonderful, caring, smiling person Chad was on the outside, none of us were able to see the torment he felt on the inside or recognize what could have been the signs of depression. Those signs can look deceptively like the all-too-common stress of young adulthood— the anxiety over finishing school, getting a job, and relationships, and the struggle to live up to expectations. We need to increase awareness and understanding of those signs, particularly in our teenagers and young adults, so that we can intervene and make sure others like Chad get the help they need. Depression is a problem that has solutions if we make it ok to talk about it, make it ok to ask for help.

I'm talking about it here, in this book about daring to dream and never downsizing your dreams, in the chance that it might help someone find the hope they need to get help for depression or mental illness. In the hope that it might bring the conversation out in the open so that we can bring those affected out of the darkness and into the light.

The loss of my son left a hole in my heart and my life that will never be filled. I miss him every single day. But I am forever grateful for the 25 amazing years I had with him. I cherish the memories and I relive them every day—I close my eyes and I can see his smile, his walk, I can hear his voice and his laugh. He gave me more joy in those 25 years than many people experience in a lifetime, and I will always feel blessed that God gave me those beautiful years and the memories that must now last me a lifetime.

What I have learned through all of these hardships and tragedies in my life is that in any challenge, whether it's obstacles at work, or tragedies in your personal life, relying on your family, friends, and faith is critical.

I could have stopped fighting, stopped pressing on, at so many different points along the way. But I kept fighting. And by the Grace of God, and through the love and support of my family, friends, and my faith, I found a way to see the joy and blessings that still remain in this life.

Every one of you will face speed bumps and twists and turns in your life and in your career.

Illness, loss, and other misfortunes will occur.

Layoffs happen. New leaders take over, changing the direction and the culture of a business.

People who have dealt with adversity in their lives become stronger, are more resilient, more creative, more adaptive, understand the need to rely on others to get the job done and get through life.

My experience has convinced me that there is absolutely nothing in this life that can't be overcome. If you can live through the loss of your only child and learn not just to survive, but to embrace life again, there is nothing that can't be conquered.

Make sure you take care of your family, friends, and faith—and they'll be there to take care of you when you need it most.

I dare you to take responsibility for your attitude, and to know that your attitude can and will determine your success and happiness in life.

Chapter 9: Don't Downsize Your Dreams

We need more women to have the confidence to dare to imagine what's possible, and then *never downsize their dreams.*

We've made undeniable progress, and there are so many positive trends that are signaling a change.

Women are more educated than ever before. In the United States they now earn more college and graduate degrees than men.

Women make up half the workforce, and we are closing the gap in middle management.

Studies show women score higher on a majority of competencies critical for executive leadership. Interestingly, the one area in which women score lower is *confidence.*

Studies show that women enter the workforce with just as much ambition as men.

And half a dozen global studies conducted by the likes of Goldman Sachs and Columbia University show that companies that have women in top executive positions and on their boards perform better than those that don't—they deliver better outcomes in terms of business and financial performance.

So the data is irrefutable, the research impossible to ignore.

And yet, we're not making as much progress as those facts would suggest.

We need more companies to understand that policies that keep women in the workforce and allow them to succeed and advance are not just good for women, they are good for business.

We need women, and their male colleagues, to have the courage to push for a workplace that allows all of us to more effectively juggle the demands of work and family in this always-on world. Because healthy minds, hearts, and families are good for business.

And we need more women to have the confidence to envision their idea of success and the conviction to pursue it, and Refuse to Downsize their Dreams.

Because I believe the possibilities are endless for those of us who have the courage to push through the obstacles, cruise over the speed bumps, and passionately pursue our own definition of success.

So now it's your turn.

It's your turn to dare to imagine your passion, your purpose, what's possible for you.

I'd like to leave you with a final thought.

When people near the end of their lives and are asked what they regret most... they consistently cite five things:

1. Not being brave enough to pursue their dreams
2. Caring too much about what other people think
3. Working too hard
4. Not spending more time with family and friends
5. Wishing they had made more of a difference

Don't let that be you. Don't look back on your life with regret for the things you didn't do. Look back on your life and know that you pursued your dream, you spent time with the important people in your life, and you made a difference.

You're reading this because you care. Because you have dreams. Because you know you're capable of great things, and you want to make a difference. Because you want to be on a stage one day, sharing your journey to success and illuminating the path for others to follow. And I know you can do it.

I'm not telling you it's going to be easy. I'm telling you it's going to be worth it.

Don't Downsize Your Dreams.

And never forget, as you climb the ladder, to reach a hand back to help others achieve their dreams, to open doors for others. There is room at the top for all of us, and when you get there it's good to have friends.

Made in the USA
Middletown, DE
25 November 2016